THE EARP PAPERS:
IN A BROTHER'S IMAGE

by
Don Chaput

Affiliated Writers of America/Publishers
Encampment, Wyoming
Printed in the United States of America

Published by

Affiliated Writers of America, Inc.
P.O. Box 343
Encampment, Wyoming 82325
1-800-292-5292

ISBN: 1-879915-10-3

Library of Congress Catalog Card Number: 94- 70540

CONTENTS

TABLE OF DOCUMENTS
AND PHOTOGRAPHS

ABOUT THE AUTHOR

Don Chaput is Curator Emeritus of the Natural History Museum in Los Angeles. He has written on all sorts of aspects of frontier history, including mining, the Army in the West, Indian affairs, exploration, and law and order. His works have appeared in such journals as *Western History Quarterly*, *Journal of San Diego History*, *Pacific Historian*, *Journal of Arizona History*, *Southern California Quarterly*, *Missouri Historical Review*, and *Louisiana History*.

He was a contributor to the *Smithsonian Handbook of North American Indians*, a consultant to the *Dictionary of Canadian Biography*, and the mining consultant to the TIME-LIFE publication *Noble Metals*.

Mr. Chaput's long association with the mining history of North America has led him to develop new perspectives on Virgil Earp and his brothers, as the Earp boys followed the gold and silver trail for forty years, as lawmen, miners, gamblers, and saloon operators, from Dakota Territory to Arizona, California, Nevada, Colorado, Idaho, Montana, and Alaska.

FOREWORD
THE EARPS: WORTH THE INK?

Was the Earp family really significant on the American frontier? Probably not. The family, although well known today, were in their own time only fringe characters. In spite of his modern reputation as a shootist of the first class, there is no hard evidence that Wyatt Earp ever killed a man. The sole episode that lends some degree of credibility occurred in the famous Tombstone shootout, where a few of Wyatt's bullets may have helped send the McLaurys into the next world. All other claims to events that have Wyatt dueling with or killing his opponents are based on conjecture. Researchers who have studied his career know this. The bullet-riddled body of Frank Stilwell was found by the railroad tracks in Tucson, and Wyatt and a few others may actually have ambushed him. And so on. Not once in his career did Wyatt Earp engage in a man-to-man duel; people get hurt that way.

The Tombstone incident provides another lesson for those seeking the truth. Wyatt Earp was not in charge and therefore made none of the major decisions on that fateful day. His brother Virgil was a Deputy U. S. Marshal and also City Marshal of

Tombstone; Virgil was in charge, set the tone, and decided what to do and when to do it as they moved towards the famous shootout.

The other two well known Earps were even less than fringe types. Warren was an insecure, high strung young man who tried to get by on his "Earpness." He was a constant trouble-maker, in Tombstone, Riverside, and Yuma, was arrested for drunkenness, fighting, and petty thievery. He died in 1900 in the obscure Arizona town of Willcox in a cheap saloon, shot in a bar fight. Morgan didn't get beyond Tombstone. He was gunned to death, shot through a saloon window while playing pool with his brother Wyatt and others.

Well, scratch Morgan and Warren as major players. That leaves Virgil and Wyatt. Virgil had a mediocre law career after being dismissed as Tombstone's City Marshal. He served as town constable of Colton, California, for a few years in the late 1880s; he also ran saloons, promoted fights, and tried for political office at least half a dozen times. He couldn't get elected as sheriff of Yavapai County, Arizona. When he ran for constable in the mining town of Vanderbilt, California, he was slaughtered at the polls. In the 1890s, while living in Prescott, he earned a few dollars as a server of summonses for the local courts. At least Virgil's last titled position sounded respectable—Deputy Sheriff of Esmeralda County, Nevada. After working a few months as a saloon bouncer, he died of pneumonia in Goldfield, Nevada, in 1905.

Wyatt had the good sense to live much longer, as he died in a modest Los Angeles bungalow in 1929. Yet, Wyatt's days before and after Tombstone were not covered in law enforcement glory. He was never top man in Wichita or Dodge City; he acted as a deputy or assistant marshal, firing an occasional bullet or two, but he spent most of his time hitting drunken Texas cowboys over the head with his pistol. His behavior after the Tombstone shootout was really bizarre. With a temporary appointment as a Deputy U. S. Marshal he went on a vendetta against those who had killed Morgan and who had tried to kill Virgil. Wyatt may have killed some people during this frenetic period; if so, it happened in the dark, without witnesses. After this, Wyatt fled to New Mexico and Colorado in disgrace.

From that period on, moving frequently, Wyatt tried horse racing, mining, ranching, running a bar in the Idaho mining country, buying real estate in San Diego, gambling and salooning in Alaska, running crap games in Los Angeles, and trying to profit from the new oil fields of Kern County, California. Apparently Wyatt's last law enforcement position was in 1902 in Nevada, where he was appointed a Deputy U. S. Marshal by the marshal of the Ninth Circuit Court; he was to serve summonses for the federal courts.

There were two older Earp boys. Newton, or "Newton the Good," was a half-brother from father Nick's earlier marriage who never had much to do with the family. He farmed for decades in central California. James Earp, oldest of the boys from Nick's second marriage, picked up a severe arm wound during the Civil War. He spent half a century in second-rate saloons in Montana, Arizona, Nevada, and California as a gambler, operator, or manager. He breathed his last in Los Angeles in 1926.

Now, these summaries may be incomplete, but they record the highlights of the careers of the Earp brothers. It is true that the Tombstone shootout of 1881 was well known, but such a single incident was not sufficient to turn the Earps into the household names they have become in the twentieth century.

Much has been written about the West, and in particular about the Earp brothers. Through dozens of movies and television productions, hundreds of books and magazine articles, each generation of the entertainment world decides to interpret the

Earps anew. But these efforts are concerned with legend, with literary and show business mystique, not with history. The Earps of the late nineteenth century are not that difficult to understand. There is evidence aplenty to place them in the collection of restless westward wanderers, following the call of new mines, better ranch lands, more opportunity. They went to these places with little or nothing. Yet, they forged into these new communities, and usually attained some type of status. In Lamar, Missouri, it would be as town constables; in Dodge City, as members of the police force; in Tombstone, Colton, Goldfield, they again wore badges.

The Earps patterned many of their interests and actions from their father, restless Nick Earp, a constable in Monmouth, Illinois, in 1857, who ended as Justice of the Peace [and saloon keeper] in Colton, California, in the 1880s; Constable Virgil Earp would arrest the drunk or tramp, and Justice Nicholas Earp would fine him.

The Earps were an interesting Western family, but their careers have been romanticized, enhanced, and widely exaggerated and publicized due to many cultural changes in America in this century. The Earps—Wyatt especially—were as far removed from the stereotype of the gunfighter as we can imagine. Yet, the evolving publishing world and the worlds of cinema and television have snatched these fellows with the short, euphonious name of Earp, elaborated on the Tombstone episode, and spun all sorts of yarns and impossible tales around this family.

The Earps were not really important people. But their importance as symbols of the American frontier heritage is impossible to exaggerate.

Therefore, a presentation of information, data, documents, letters, and other evidence seems not only justified but worthwhile. These men, who have become so prominent for things they did not do, deserve to be known for what they really were. We can look at this evidence from different viewpoints, and maybe we can find the reality behind the legends.

There are no bulging boxes of Earp Papers anywhere, but there are hundreds of Earp letters and documents in the Huntington Library, the Arizona Historical Society, and the Seaver Center for Western History Research at the Natural History Museum, Los Angeles. Scattered throughout the libraries, archives, and museums of the world there are thousands of additional documents, letters, photographs, and published materials about the Earps. It would be possible to publish a five-volume set of such material, if any need for such a publication existed. Assembled here are key pieces of information that enable us to follow the Earps throughout their many careers, in their numerous, wide-ranging communities. The materials presented are all identified as to source, and a bibliography discusses where this and other material can be located.

Many institutions provided material for this work, or facilitated research in their archives, libraries, and museums. Yet, the most profitable information and perspectives have come from Lee Silva, a solid researcher on the West and the Earps, and Carl Chafin, who has spent decades absorbing the primary sources related to Tombstone and southern Arizona. They are ideal researchers: they accumulate, interpret, and share.

CHAPTER 1
FAMILY BACKGROUND

SOME EARP FAMILY HISTORY

Earp Genealogy, courtesy of the Warren County Library, Monmouth, Illinois. Abstracts and excerpts follow.

John Earpe, born c. 1600, Staffordshire, England

Thomas Earpe, Sr., born 1631, Lurgan, Ireland; died c. 1700, Derbyshire, England.

Thomas Earp, Jr., born 1665, barony of Fews, Ireland, first Earp to America, died about 1720.

John Earp [1680-1744], in 1728 moved to Fairfax County, Virginia, apparently died there. He married Rebecca [?], had sons William, America, and Joshua.

Joshua [1700-1755], married Mary Budd, sold Potomac River land in 1737, bought land in Virginia; had sons William, Caleb, and Matthew.

William, born 1729, married Priscilla Nichols in 1752, had nine children, including Phillip.

Phillip, born 1755 Fairfax County, served in American Revolution, had sons Walter and Nimrod, wife's name unknown. He died in North Carolina.

Walter Earp, born 1787, Montgomery County, Maryland. Married Martha Early in 1809. Moved to North Carolina, Lincoln County, where their first three of nine children were born.

Nicholas Porter Earp, born in Lincoln County, North Carolina, September 6, 1813; father of the "Fighting Earps."

*   *   *

Portion of newspaper article, Monmouth Daily Review Atlas, February 16, 1956, in Archives, Central College, Pella, Iowa. Martha and Walter Earp were the grandparents of the "fighting Earps."

Martha Earp was born in North Carolina Aug. 28, 1790 (family name Early). She was married to Walter Earp in 1809. They both professed religion and joined the Methodist Episcopal church. In the fall of 1813 Walter Earp and his wife and their three children, the youngest being an infant, emigrated to Kentucky stopping in Tennessee for two or three years, somewhere near the Cumberland river. They then moved to Kentucky and settled in Russellville, Logan County, where Mr. Earp taught school a few years, then to Morgan Town, Butler County, where he taught several more years. He was a school teacher by profession, also a licensed preacher in the M. E. church. From Butler County he moved to Ohio County, improved a farm and lived there about 20 years. They raised all their children born to them, lived to see all married

2

and settled in life. In the year 1847 Mr. Earp, his wife and their sons and daughters with the families moved from Kentucky to Illinois, settling in Monmouth, Warren County. Mr. Earp lived about 6 years after they moved here and died in the city of Mommouth in the 66th year of his age. Martha Earp lived to be a good old age and died on the 24th of September (1881) in the city of Monmouth, Warren County, being 91 years and 27 days old.

*   *   *

Earp Family Bible entries, provided by Archives, Central College, Pella, Iowa.

Births:

Nicholas P. Earp was born Sept. 6th in the year of our Lord 1813

Abigail Storm was born Sept. 21st in the year of our Lord 1813

Newton J. Earp, first born of Nicholas P. Earp and his wife Abigail was born Oct. 7th in the year of our Lord 1837

Mariah Ann Earp, second born of N. P. Earp and his wife Abigail was born Feb. 12 in the year of our Lord 1839

James C. Earp, first born of N. P. Earp and Virginia his wife was born June 28, 1841

Virgil W. Earp was born July 18th in the year of our Lord 1843

Martha E. Earp was born Sept. 25, 1845

Wyatt B. S. Earp was born March 19, 1848

Morgan W. Earp was born April 24, 1851

Baxter W. Earp was born March 9, 1855

Virginia Ann Earp was born Feb. 26, 1858

Adelia E. Earp was born June 16, 1861

The Earp family lived in, and Wyatt Earp was born in this Monmouth, Illinois, home in 1848. Wyatt Earp Birthplace Museum

Marriages:

Nicholas P. Earp and Abigail Storm were married on the 22nd
day of Dec. A. D. 1836

Nicholas P. Earp and Virginia Ann Cooksey were married on
July 30, 1840 [She was born Feb. 2, 1821.]

Deaths:

Abigail Earp, first wife of N. P. Earp departed this life Oct. 8,
1839

Mariah Ann Earp, dau. of N. P. Earp and his wife Abigail,
departed this life on the 5th of Jan. 1839, aged 10 mo, 1
day

Martha Elizabeth Earp, dau. of N. P. Earp and V. A. Earp his
wife, departed this life on the 26th of May 1856, aged 10
years, 8 mo. and 1 day.

*   *   *

**Nicholas P. Earp married Virginia Ann Cooksey, who
became the mother of the famous Earp boys. Some of her
family history follows, extracted from Earp file, Warren
County Library, Monmouth, Illinois.**

Thomas Smith, mar. Melcenia Victoria Week, c. 1797, moved
from Virginia to Ohio Co., Ky., 1817;

Elizabeth Smith, born Jan., 1800, Virginia, married James
Cooksey in 1817 (He was son of Phillip Cooksey of
Fauquier Co., Virginia); James Cooksey & wife Elizabeth
moved to Ohio Co., Ky., in 1817, as part of a party of 87
persons, 14 horses, a chest of gold coins, and a wedding
dress from Europe embroidered with pearls; both were

wealthy members of the old Virginia Aristocracy. James died in 1828 in a logging accident.

Virginia Ann Cooksey, born February 2, 1823 (or, perhaps 1821), on July 30, 1840, married Nicholas Porter Earp.

*   *   *

NICK, THE MEXICAN WAR VETERAN
Pension File, National Archives.

MEXICAN WAR SURVIVOR: United States of America, Department of the Interior, Bureau of Pensions.

I certify that in conformity with the laws of the United States, approved January 29, 1887, and January 5, 1893, Nicholas P. Earp, late a Sergeant, Captain W. B. Stapp's Company, Illinois Mounted Volunteers, is entitled to pension at the rate of Twelve dollars per month to commence on the Twentieth day of April one thousand eight hundred and ninety-four. Issued in lieu of certificate dated May 19, 1894, to correct date of commencement of increase.

Fourth day of January, one thousand nine hundred and two
/s/ Ethan A. Hitchcock, Secretary of the Interior

Adjutant General's Office, Washington, D.C., April 18, 1877
Sir: I have the honor to acknowledge the receipt from your Office of application for Pension No. Mexican War, and to return it herewith, with such information as is furnished by the files of this Office.

It appears from the Rolls on file in this Office that Nicholas P. Earp was enrolled on the 7 day of June, 1847, at Monmouth Ills., in Capt. Stapp's company of Illinois Mounted Volunteers, to serve during the war with Mexico and mustered into service as a Sergeant on the 10 day of August, 1847, at Quincy Ills., in Capt.

Stapp's Co. of Illinois Mounted Volunteers, to serve during the war with Mexico. On the Muster Roll of the Company for the months of Sept.-Oct.-Nov.-Dec., 1847, he is reported Sergt. Sick in Hospl. at Vera Cruz. Muster out roll dated July 15, 1848, reported him discharged at Vera Cruz Decr. 24, 1847.

From Nicholas P. Earp Pension File, Central College, Pella, Iowa.

I received a specific disability occasioned by the kick of a mule in my groin from which I have never recovered, this disability being received at Magdelena, Mexico while in active service in the Mexican War for my country.

The following is a portion of the widow's application for pension support, filed by Annie Earp, 1900 West 7th St., San Bernardino, California.

My former husband Ambrose P. Alexander rendered no service in the Army or Navy of the United States. My second and last husband, the said Nicholas P. Earp was a survivor of the Mexican War and drew a pension for such service up to the time of his death. I heard him say that he was in the Black Hawk War, but know that he drew his pension for service in the Mexican War. His marriage to his wife Virginia Ann Earp was his first marriage and she died here in San Bernardino California January 14th 1893, and is buried here. He never married except with me which was on October 14th, 1893.

*   *   *

THE ILLINOIS-IOWA CONNECTION

Wyatt Earp was born in Monmouth, Illinois, on March 19, 1848. The following is one of the many statements regarding the home in which he was born, collected in order to verify that fact; Wyatt Earp Birthplace Museum, Monmouth.

My grandparents, Josiah and Elizabeth Allen Earp, lived at 213 South Third Street, Monmouth, Illinois. Wyatt Earp was not born in my grandparents home.

I am one of the four living second cousins of Wyatt. The other three are—my brother Charles of rural Galesburg, my brother Lawrence of Moscow, Iowa, and Jeanette Kneen Boock who is a descendant of Sarah Earp Eby. Jeanette is in a nursing home in Monmouth, Ill.

My Uncle Alfred Levi Earp, who was born in 1852, said Wyatt Earp was born at 406 South Third Street in the house where my cousin Anna Stratton lived. I had no reason to doubt him.

I firmly believe Wyatt was born at 406 South Third Street, Monmouth, Illinois.

Effie Earp Cramer, January 27, 1988

*   *   *

Census of 1850, Township of Lake Prairie, County of Marion, Iowa; from Archives, Central College, Pella, Iowa.

N. P. Earp	37	North Carolina cooper & farmer
Virginia A. Earp	29	Kentucky
Newton J. Earp	13	" "
James C. Earp	7	" "

8

Virgil W. Earp	6	"
Martha E. Earp	5	Illinois
Wyatt B. Earp	2	"

*   *   *

From 1857 Galesburg, Monmouth, Knoxville and Abingdon Directory, portion of page 108, courtesy of Wyatt S. Earp Birthplace Museum, Monmouth, Illinois.

Earp, Nicholas P. constable, Court H. h West av. cor Illinois
Earp, Walter C. Water cor Illinois

*   *   *

From Monmouth, Nick Earp moved the family to Pella, Iowa. The following incidents relate to the Civil War years there; from "History of Pella," provided by Central College Archives, Pella.

Wyatt, then just 13 years and his two younger brothers aged 10 and 6, were left at home to cultivate and harvest 80 acres of corn. The second spring of the war brought the same work to be done. One morning young Wyatt laid down his hoe and, thinking his father was in the western part of the county, headed for Ottumwa to try to enlist. Great was his chagrin when almost the first person he met was his father—who quickly sent him back to the cornfield.

The year 1863 found Nicholas Earp still firmly opposed to secession, but unable actively to support the Northern determination to free the slaves, so he resigned from army service. Since his sons disagreed with his views, he insisted it was their duty to

9

continue in the Union Army. James was sent home in '63 after receiving a severe wound, but Newton and Virgil served until the end of the war.

While Nicholas was training troops during the war he also served as Alderman of First Ward, Pella, and later was appointed Marshal, which position he held until he left Pella as captain of a wagon train to California in the spring of 1864.

* * *

While at Pella, Nicholas Earp owned some town lots, and worked acreage on the outskirts of Pella. The following land data is from the Earp File, Archives, Central College, Pella.

N. P. Earp, deed, 40 acres, NW 1/4 of SE 1/4, of 1/77/18: 1855
 " , deed, 40 acres, SW 1/2 of NE 1/4, of 1/77/18: 1859
 " , deed, 80 acres, SE 1/4 of NE 1/4, &
NE 1/4 of SE 1/4: 1859
 " , deed, 160 acres, S 1/2 NE 1/4 and
N 1/2 SSE 1/4, 1/77/18: 1856

* * *

Census of 1860, Town of Pella, Lake Prairie Township, Marion County, Iowa; from Archives, Central College, Pella.

Nicholas Earp	45	N.C.	farmer
Virginia A. Earp	38	Ky	
James C. Earp	19	"	
Virgil W. Earp	17	"	

For several years in the 1850s the Nicholas Earp family lived in this brick structure in Pella, Iowa, on E. Franklin Street. Central College Archives, Pella

Wyatt Earp	12	Ill
Morgan Earp	9	Iowa
Warren B. Earp	5	Iowa
Virginia A. Earp	2	Ill
Lucinda Davis	17	Ky

*   *   *

THE EARPS GO TO WAR

Virgil's military record, in the National Archives, shows that he enrolled July 26, 1862, as a private in what became Company C, 83rd Illinois Infantry Regiment; he was mustered out and discharged on June 26, 1865, as a private, at Nashville, Tennessee.

Remarks: Stoppage for one Remington revolver lost or stolen $20.00. Stoppage of 1/2 months pay by sentence Reg. C. M. Gen. Post Order No. 9, Hd. Qrs. 5, Sub Dist. Mid. Tenn. Apr 15/65.

*   *   *

The following details are from the Muster Roll, Company C, 83rd Regiment of Illinois Volunteers, Illinois State Archives.

Earp, Virgil W., age 19, 5' 10", light hair, blue eyes, light complexion, single, farmer, born Morgan County, Ky. Joined regt. July 26, 1862, Monmouth, for 3 yrs. Mustered in Aug. 21, Monmouth, by Capt. Christopher. Residence—Pella, Marion Cty, Iowa. Mustered out, June 24, 1865, at Nashville, by Capt. Chickering.

*   *   *

A summary of Newton's Civil War service, from Archives, Central College, Pella.

Newton J. Earp - Civil War - age 24 years, Residence: Pella. Nativity, Ky. Enlisted 11 Nov. 1861 in Co. F, Fourth Cavalry, Iowa Volunteers. Mustered: 23 Nov. 1863. Promoted 1 Sept. 1863 to Seventh Corporal. Re-enlisted and remustered 12 Dec. 1863. Promoted 1 Jan. 1864 to Sixth Corporal; 1 Jan. 1865 to Fourth Corporal. Mustered out: 26 June 1865, Louisville, Ky.

*   *   *

FIRST TRAIL WEST

In 1864 a party of settlers left Pella, Iowa, for California, led by wagonmaster Nicholas P. Earp. Virgil was still in the Union Army, but James, the wounded war veteran, Wyatt, Morgan, Warren, Adelia, and Mrs. Earp were part of the westward trek, headed for San Bernardino. The wife of Dr. J. A. Rousseau kept a diary, and a few excerpts follow. She did not care for Nick Earp; Nick was a stern wagonmaster, but his methods were apparently the correct ones. There were no major problems, and all in the party arrived safely at their destination. From, San Bernardino Museum Association Quarterly, VI, winter, 1968.

We are now on top of the hill or rather mountain and I must acknowledge I never saw such a one, let alone ascend it. When we were below the worst part of it, I looked up and thought it an utter impossibility for any animal to get up. Toward the top there was

13

a perpendicular rock some six feet to get up, besides some others not so bad. We all doubled teams but Mr. Earp's wagon. He started up that awful mountain with our mare and Mr. Hamilton started a span of mules after them to help them get along, they got up safely. It appeared to me he didn't care if he killed our horses or not. If he had he wouldn't have tried to go with only two. . . .

This evening Mr. Earp had another rippet with Warren fighting with Jimmy Hatten. And then he commenced about all the children. Used very profane language and swore if the children's parents did not whip or correct their children he would whip every last one of them. He still shows out more and more every day what kind of a man he is. . . .

Another clear pleasant morning, but cool. Making ready to leave camp, have plenty of Indians around all the time. I am tired out seeing them. Mr. Earp has just given up our box of books, says he can't take them any farther. So we'll leave them at this place to be taken by some freighters the first opportunity. Charlie Coply has left Mr. Earp and going the remaining part of the way with us.

*   *   *

In April of 1865, Nick Earp wrote a long, rambling, sometimes incomprehensible letter of his adventures across the plains to James Coplea of Pella. The following, from the Earp Papers, Archives, Central College, Pella, displays Nick's narrative style, and portrays one of the incidents on the Westward trek.

We had not bin in camp long untell the Sentinels gave the alarm that the Indians was coming so I ordered the horses to be brought inside the corell by the gards that was garding them the women all turned out to help get the horses into the corell while we who

14

Nicholas Earp, father of the "Fighting Earps," held such positions as constable, wagon master, and justice of the peace, in Illinois, Missouri, across the Plains, and in California. Natural History Museum, Los Angeles

was not on gard gethered our guns and rushed to meet the Indians when they got as clos as we entended them to come we commenced poping away at them and soon succeeded in checking them and puting them to flite they ran off about a half a mile and stoped and turned round as tho they war not satisfied.

I said boys they are not satisfied lets satisfy them so I ran to the waggons and jumped upon a horse and said we'll make them leave there. Dr. Rusau T. J. Ellis James Earp and a young man by name of Tucker that was with Hamiltons and two other men that got in with us followed suit and off we charged after the Indians when they saw we war making for them they wheeled about and off they pout on we went in full persuit of them untell they found were about to over take them then faced about to gave us battle they were about 4 to one of us I gave order to form a line of battle and we went into a general engagement they undertook to flank us first to the right and then to the left, but they found out they couldn't for they had their match.

So they then began to give back the arrows flew and the bullets whised they began to gave back to keep out of range of our guns we rushed on when Dr. Rusau put his mareen glasses to his eyes and descovered the man who seemed to be leading the band gaving command was a white man he hollowed out Earp shoot that man on the roan horse he is a white man as I was closest to them I leveled on him and at the crack of the gun he fell to ons side of the horse but caught in the mane and recovered again then wheeled his horse and lumbered over the hill as fast as his horse would take him the rest immediately took to flight following him we had exhausted all our shots.

*   *   *

James accompanied the wagon train to Nevada, where

16

he stopped for some time. The following incident is from the Adelia Earp Edwards Memoirs, Colton Public Library.

One tale I remember well, Jim used to tell, and we all used to poke a little fun at him about it all. I was just a little baby at the time and Jim had gone off to a mining town at Austin, Nevada. One night, he was going home after a time out with the boys when all of a sudden there rose up out of the night right there in front of him, a strange looking giant beast, snarling and hissing. It was a camel. Maybe Jim didn't find out that it was a camel just then, he just "sort of wandered back to the boys," as he used to say. There were quite a few camels in that part of the desert then. They had been used for work in the desert and some got loose and would wander about and turned up here and there. Jim called strong drink "Camel juice" after that and always did.

*   *   *

Records are skimpy about the doings of Virgil and Wyatt in the late 1860s. The following paragraphs are from the Adelia Earp Edwards Memoir. Supposedly, Virgil and maybe Wyatt, had been stage drivers or stage hands on a Los Angeles-San Bernardino-Prescott-Salt Lake City run. Only Virgil's role in these events seem to merit serious attention.

When Virgil finished stage driving he and Wyatt went to Prescott, working for a big San Bernardino freight company with great wagons and long teams of mules and oxen. When they arrived in Prescott, all the men went to a saloon in town to celebrate a mite. Wyatt had hardly taken a drink before and the whiskey soon had him reeling. Real drunk. He just passed on out and Virgil and another friend took him off to his bed. When he

17

woke up, he was in a terrible state alright, sick, headache, perspiring and trembling all over. Virge told him the only cure was to take a few more drinks. He did just that, and got just as bad as before. By the time he was close to sobering up, it was time for that rough old return journey and he suffered so bad for a day or two he swore not to touch whiskey again. And he kept to that for twenty years! But he would take a couple of glasses of beer or wine most days, but that was about all.

*   *   *

FARMING AND LAWING IN MISSOURI

The following documents of the Earps in Lamar, Barton County, Missouri, are in the manuscripts collection, State Historical Society of Missouri, Columbia.

(1869, November 17)
Now at this day comes N. P. Earp and offers his resignation as Constable of Lamar Township, which resignation is by the Court accepted.

Ordered by the Court that Wyatt S. EARP be and is hereby appointed Constable of Lamar Township, Barton County and that he be commissioned as such.

Ordered by the Court that N. P. Earp be and he is hereby appointed Justice of the Peace within and for Lamar Township, Barton County and that he be commissioned as such.

Inquest, Jury fees, May 3rd, 1870.

| Wm. B. Smedley | Jury fees | $1.00 |
| J. Alter | " | 1.00 |

D. Bingham	"	1.00
G. Young	"	1.00
N. P. Earp	"	1.00
John Ford	"	1.00
Wyatt S. Earp	Constable	6.00

1870.

This is to certify that I have this day united in marriage Mr. W. S Earp and Miss Urilla Sutherland. N. P. Earp
Justice of the Peace
Filed and Recorded Jan. 24th, 1870

1870.

Lamar, Missouri, May 28th 1870. This is to Certify that I have united together in Marriage Mr. V W Earp and Miss Rozilia Draggoo, May 30th 1870. N P Earp, J P
Filed for Record May 30th 1870

1870, December 21.

Now at this day comes N. P. Earp Justice of the Peace and presents bill of costs in Case of the State of Missouri vs Samuel Jones, Theodore Edwards, and Joseph Graham, and it appearing to the Court that the County is liable for the costs in said case and the Court finding said bill correct, it is ordered that the same be allowed and warrants issue as follows towit:

N. P. Earp	Justice	$6,00
W. S. Earp	Constable	14.00
Hatfield	Witness-2 days	1.00

John J. Humphrey	"	1.00
J. Homan	"	1.00
L. Homan	"	1.00
J. W. Dunn	"	1.00

1871, March 17.

On this day it is ordered that Wyatt S. Earp be allowed the sum of thirty eight dollars & fifty five cents for services rendered as Constable in cases of State of Missouri against Macklin Grummet & others.

The following incident with Wyatt as Lamar constable appeared in a Lamar newspaper in June 16, 1870, and was reprinted on p. 95 of Turner, The Earps Talk.

One of our citizens had a brother from a distance call to see him on Monday last, and having not seen each other for a long time, they started around town to have a good time, generally. Taking aboard a good supply of "forty rod," they wandered around town until evening when Constable Earp found one of them upon the street incapable of taking care of himself and took him down to a stone building which he has appropriated for use of just such customers. As Mr. Earp was about turning the key upon his bird, the other came staggering up enquiring for his brother. Mr. Earp opened the door and slid him in. Coming up the square, Mr. Earp met another hard case in the shape of a tramping butcher, who asked Mr. Earp to purchase him a pencil in place of one he alleged Mr. Earp had borrowed of him some time previous. Mr. Earp enticed him down to the stone building to procure him a pencil, and of course he shared the fate of the other two. There being a hole in the roof of the building the three caged birds managed to crawl out before morning, and the stranger not liking the reception he met with here, left for parts unknown. The other two were brought before Esq. Earp [Wyatt's father, Nicholas P. Earp, Justice of the Peace], and fined $5 and costs, each. A few more examples, and the town will be better for it.

United States Census, 1870, Barton County, Missouri.

Earp, Nicholas P	38 [57]	grocer b. N. Carolina
Earp, Virginia	50	keeping hs. b. Kentucky
Earp, Warren	13	b. Iowa
Earp, Adelia	9	
Earp, Virgil	26	grocer b. Kentucky
Earp, Newton	33	farmer b. Kentucky
Earp, Nancy	24	keeping hs. b. Kentucky
Earp, Effie	2/12	b. Missouri

The following Barton County Court record of January 18, 1871, concerns Wyatt's father-in-law, William Sutherland, a local hotel owner.

Now at this day comes William Sutherland and presents his account against Barton County for boarding prisoner 24 days and the premises being seen it is ordered by the Court that the said William Sutherland be allowed $1.25 per day for boarding said prisoner, making in all $30.00 and that a warrant issue therefore.

*　　*　　*

THE OTHER SIDE OF THE LAW

What Wyatt did after he left Lamar is not completely

clear. Ed Bartholomew uncovered many documents from a horse theft case that appear to explain some of Wyatt's whereabouts, although Bartholomew confuses the evidence, and reluctantly admits that Wyatt was never apprehended nor tried; from Bartholomew, Untold Story.

Whereas at the District Court of the United States of America, for the Western District of Arkansas, at the May Term, began and holden in the city of Fort Smith on the 8th of May AD 1871, the Grand Jurors, in and for said District, empanneled, brought into the said Court a True Bill of Indictment against Wyatt Earp and John Shown for Larceny in the Indian Country against the peace and dignity of the United States. And by the said indictment, now remaining on file and of record in said Court will ------appear, to which indict Said Wyatt Earp and John Shown has not yet appeared or pleaded. Now therefore, You are hereby commanded in the name of the PRESIDENT of the United States of America, to apprehend said Earp and Shown and him to detain, and, bring before the said court at the Untied States Court Room, in the city of Fort Smith, in said District, at the November Term thereof, to be held on the 13 or 18th day of November AD 1871, to answer Said Indictment.

/S/ Judge, Wm Storys

Testimony of Anna Shown, wife of John Shown.

I know Wyatt S. Earp and Ed Kennedy. They got my husband drunk near Ft. Gibson, I. T. about the 28th of March 1871. They went and got Mr. Jim Keys Horses, and put my husband on one and he lead the other, and told him to ride 50 miles towards Kansas and then they would hitch the horses to a wagon and he could ride. I went with these two men and met my husband 50 miles North of Fort Gibson, and I rode with these two men in a hack, on meeting my husband they took the two horses out of the hack and put in the two that he had. Earp Drove on towards Kansas for three full nights (We laid over Days). About 3 o'clock of the 3d night James M. Keys overtook us. My husband John Shown said he could have the horses-the other Defts. Earp and Kennedy told Keys that my husband Stole the horses. They also said that if Shown (My husband) turned States Evidence then they would kill him.

*   *   *

LIFE ON THE FRONTIER

Here are some insights into the personalities of Morgan and Newton Earp, provided in the memoirs of Adelia Earp Edwards.

Morgan was in a fight with a buffalo hunter [1870s] one day there and it would have come to shooting if Newton had not gotten between them and talked them into shaking hands. Morgan had a terrible temper while Newton was always very even in his ways. I recall he used to say, "Morg and Warren will be the death of me." And my father said, "Yes, they're like to shoot you." But when they had shooting matches, Newton and Virgil would always win. They were very good shots, trained by the army. . .

We lived awhile near Newton and his family in Kansas while we arranged things for going to California. Newton was a quiet, hard-working man and always a leader in the communities they lived. His wife and his mother-in-law were fine, hard-working ladies, too. They had very strong moral characters and were very religious. Real old-day strict Methodists. Mother and a few others

23

thought they were just that bit too religious. Sort of religious maniacs. We were all trying to be good Christians but we never did match up to Newton's family.

*   *   *

Virgil Earp was driving stage in Iowa-Nebraska in the early 1870s, when he met Alvira Sullivan, to be his life-long companion. The following is her account, from Waters, Earp Brothers.

There I was waitin' tables at the Planters House in Council Bluffs when I first saw him. It was early in the evenin' before most customers came in, and I had just sat down with all the other girls and some chambermaids to have our supper first. I don't know why I remember him comin' in the door so plain. He was tall, just over six feet, and had a red mustache. But anyway I asked who he was.

A "Man called Virgil Earp," said one of the girls. "He's drivin' a stage."

Virge saw me too. He always said I was just gettin' ready to take a bite out of a pickle when he first saw me. When I was mean he used to say I was just as sour. But mostly he said I was not much bigger than a pickle but a lot more sweet.

It was funny how I remembered him all the time. I can't say I liked him particularly right off. For one thing, he wasn't the looks of a man I'd figured to fall in love with. I'd always fancied somebody my own size. But Virge was handsome, and he always sat straight on a horse.

*   *   *

24

VIRGIL GOES WEST

Virgil and wife Allie Earp arrived in Prescott in the autumn of 1877. Almost immediately, Virgil was drawn into a shooting scrape which made him a well known frontier personality. Several desperadoes shot up a saloon, then tried to flee town. Three men having a chat were brought into play: Yavapai County Sheriff Ed Bowers, U. S. Marshal W. W. Standifer, and citizen Virgil Earp. The desperadoes were chased by eight or nine men, trapped, and gunned down. The Arizona Miner of October 19, 1877, has a detailed account of the shootout, and includes the following prose.

Instead of surrendering they opened fire upon the officers, which seems to have been gallantly returned both by Bowers and Murray from one direction and Standifer and McCall from the other, and in the meantime Earp, who appears to have been playing a lone hand with a Winchester rifle was doing good service between the two fires.

*   *   *

Arizona Miner, March 29, 1878; stage driver Virgil Earp was a frequent deliverer of news to the two Prescott newspapers, and the following notice is a typical example.

Mr. Earp tells us that the mill at Gillett works better and better as the machinery wears smooth, and the operators become better acquainted with its management. Several days yet remain to fill up the first month's run, yet about thirty thousand dollars in fine

*Virgil Earp was one of the most popular stage drivers when
he worked for this outfit in 1878.* Prescott Enterprise, April 24,
1878

silver and gold bullion have passed through Prescott for San
Francisco thus far, and no doubt that by the end of the month it
will approximate fifty thousand.

*　　*　　*

**Virgil's first law enforcement job in Arizona Territory;
from Prescott Enterprise, September 4, 1878.**

Resignation of W. W. Vanderbilt as night watchman of the Village, was read and accepted, and on motion of Robert Connell, Mr. Earp was appointed in his stead.

*   *   *

Prescott Enterprise, October 5, 1878.

Some good shooting was done at the gallery, yesterday, the best scores being made by Charley Spencer, and Mr. Earp, each making 44, out of a possible 45.

*   *   *

Election results, from Prescott Enterprise, November 9, 1878.

For Constable
V. W. Earp	386
Frank Murray	271
Pard Pierce	263

*   *   *

While Virgil ran a sawmill operation near Prescott, he had several encounters with prospectors and miners. The following news notes, from the Arizona Miner of October 3 and 24, 1879, suggest that Shultz was a miner who forgot to tell Virgil he was about to enter his land.

Frank Shultz came to town this afternoon from the hills west of Prescott pretty badly bruised about the head. He informs us that

Messrs. Earp and Hanson joined their forces and made an assault on him with a pistol and a large stick of wood and succeeded in getting the best of him. We believe Shultz swore out a warrant for their arrest.

Frank Shultz, the veritable Frank, has discovered another rich, gold mine in the vicinity of Lee's American Ranch. Gold can be seen in all the rock, and Col. Bean, who is located, of course, thinks it is a valuable find. **[Court records do not indicate any further action of Shultz against Virgil Earp.]**

*   *   *

Near the end of Virgil's stay in Prescott, he became ensnared in a legal tangle with one Robert Roggen. Virgil, as Constable, had been directed to force Roggen to pay his bills, by whatever means he saw fit. He applied pressure, not to the liking of the court. The following excerpt, from Roggen vs. Earp, is dated December 19, 1879, and is in the Yavapai County Court files, State Archives, Phoenix.

This cause having come on regularly to be tried was tried by the Court sitting as a jury, and having been submitted to the Court, the Court now finds the facts as follows:

That there was a sufficient delivery of the wagon described in plaintiffs complaint to take it out of the Statute of Frauds relative to the Creditors of a vendor; but is to the remainder of the property in plaintiff's complaint described there was no such sufficient delivery.

That while the sale of said property, the wagon excepted, was not good as against the creditors of the vendor, yet as between the

Vendor and Vendee it was a good and valid sale.

That the defendant failed to show that said sale was in fraud of condition and failed to show any justification of his seizure of said property or any part thereof, as constable of Prescott Precinct, or otherwise.

As a conclusion of law the Court finds that the plaintiff is entitled to the possession of said property as against the defendant. **[In other words, Virgil, starting from a position of correctness, got carried away and sold more of Roggen's possessions than was justified.]**

*   *   *

WYATT JOINS THE FORCES OF GOOD

Parts of the years 1874-77 were spent by Wyatt in Wichita; he was officially enrolled on the police force in April of 1875. The following incident, from the Wichita City Eagle of October 29, 1874, concerns an episode outside the city limits, and Wyatt seems to have been acting as a private policeman.

The Higgenbottom outfit, who attempted to jump the country at an expense of twenty or thirty thousand dollars to Wichita, it appears had, among other games, stuck M. R. Moser for a new wagon, who instead of putting himself in communication, by telegraphy, with the outside world just got two officers, John Behrens and Wiatt Erp, to light out upon the trail. These boys fear nothing and fear nobody. They made about seventy-five miles from sun to sun, across trackless prairies, striking the property and the thieves near the Indian line. To make a long and exciting story short, they just levelled a shotgun and six-shooter upon the

29

scalawags as they lay concealed in some brush, and told them to "dough over," which they did, to the amount of $146, one of them remarking that he was not going to die for the price of a wagon. It is amusing to hear Moser tell how slick the boys did the work.

Wichita Weekly Beacon, May 12, 1875.

AN ARISTOCRATIC HORSE THIEF On Tuesday evening of last week, policeman Erp, in his rounds ran across a chap whose general appearance and get up answered to a description given of one W. W. Compton, who was said to have stolen two horses and a mule from the vicinity of Le Roy, in Coffey county. Erp took him in tow, and inquired his name. He gave it as "Jones." This didn't satisfy the officer, who took Mr. Jones into the Gold Room, on Douglass avenue, in order that he might fully examine him by lamp light. Mr. Jones not liking the looks of things, lit out, running to the rear of Denison's stables. Erp fired one shot across his poop deck to bring him to, to use a naughty-cal phrase, and just as he did so, the man cast anchor near a clothes line, hauled down his colors and surrendered without firing a gun. The officer laid hold of him before he could recover his feet for another run, and taking him to jail placed him in the keeping of the sheriff.

*   *   *

While Wyatt and James Earp were in Wichita, several "girls," carrying the name Earp, were regularly arrested and fined for prostitution. Either of the brothers could have been "running the girls," as both of them engaged in such activities later in places like Dodge City, Tombstone, and

Nome. The following is a small portion of the prostitution information presented in Bartholomew, Untold Story.

State of Kansas, County of Sedgwick. Vs: In Justice's Court, Before D. A. Mitchell, a Justice of the Peace in and for Wichita City Township.

State of Kansas, Plft. Vs: Sallie and Bettsey Erp, deft. Saml. A. Martin, Prosecutor. Personally appeared before me Samuel A. Martin who being duly sworn deposes and says; that on the 3rd day of June 1874 at the County of Sedgwick and State of Kansas, one Sallie Erp and Betsey Erp did then and there unlawfully and feloniously set up and keep a bawdy house or brothel and did appear and act as mistress and have the care and management of a certain one story frame building situated and located North of Douglas Avenue near the bridge leading across the Arkansas River used and kept by such parties as a house of prostitution in this city of Wichita, County and State aforesaid contrary to the Statutes of Kansas.

*   *   *

Wyatt, after a brief career on the Wichita police force, parted on a sour note, caused by a dispute with his bosses over Wyatt's efforts to have his brothers Morgan and James on the force. He spent parts of the years 1877-79 on the Dodge City police force. The following are a few comments from that era.

Dodge City Times, July 7, 1877.

Wyatt Earp, who was on our city police force last summer, is in town again. We hope he will accept a position on the force once more. He had a quiet way of taking the most desperate characters into custody which invariably gave one the impression that the city was able to enforce her mandates and preserve her dignity. It wasn't considered policy to draw a gun on Wyatt unless you got the drop and meant to burn powder without any preliminary talk.

Dodge City Times, May 11, 1878.

Mr. Wyatt Earp, who has during the past served with credit on the police arrived in this city from Texas last Wednesday. We predict that his services as an officer will again be required this Summer.

Ford County Globe, May 14, 1878.

Wyatt Earp, one of the most efficient officers Dodge ever had, has just returned from Fort Worth, Texas. He was immediately appointed Asst. Marshal, by our City dads, much to their credit.

Dodge City Times, June 8, 1878.

Regular meeting of the city of Dodge City, held Tuesday, June 4th, 1878.

Present—James H. Kelley, Mayor; D. D. Colley, James Anderson, Walter Straeter, John Newton, Councilmen.

Absent—C. M. Beeson.

Minutes of previous meeting read and approved.

The following bills were allowed.

Chas. E. Bassett salary as Marshal	100.00
Wyatt Earp, salary as assis't Marshal	75.00
John Brown salary as Policeman	75.00
Chas Trask salary as Policeman	52.50

Same issue, same page, advertisement for the Wyatt Earp friend, Doc Holliday.

DENTISTRY

J. H. Holliday, Dentist, very respectfully offers his professional services to the citizens of Dodge City and surrounding country during the summer. Office at room No. 24, Dodge House. Where satisfaction is not given money will be refunded.

Bat Masterson and Wyatt Earp. Arizona Historical Society

34

CHAPTER 2
TO TOMBSTONE

VIRGIL'S FEDERAL BADGE

The following is Virgil's appointment as Deputy United States Marshal, from the Fred Dodge Papers, Huntington Library, San Marino, California. Virgil had received the appointment from U. S. Marshal Crawley P. Dake in Prescott, Arizona Territory, which was in Yavapai County. The following document had the name of Yavapai County stricken out, replaced by Pima County. Enroute to Tombstone, Virgil had stopped in Tucson, seat of Pima County, where his commission was re-issued.

Territory of Arizona, County of Pima: I, V. W. Earp, do solemnly swear that I will support the Constitution of the United States and the laws of this Territory; that I will true faith and

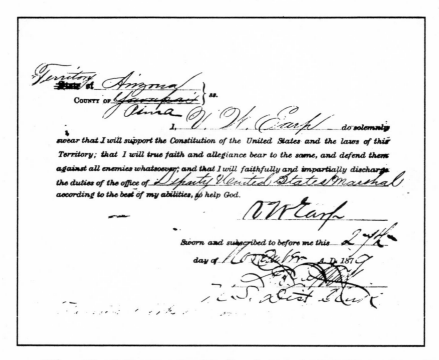

When Virgil Earp arrived in Tombstone in late November of 1879, he was carrying the authority of a Deputy U.S. Marshal. This is his oath of office. Fred Dodge Collection, Huntington Library

allegiance bear to the same, and defend them against all enemies whatsoever; and that I will faithfully and impartially discharge the duties of the office of Deputy United States Marshal according to the best of my abilities, so help God.

/S/ V W Earp

Sworn and subscribed to before me this 27th
day of November A. D. 1879
(signature illegible)

* * *

36

NEW EARP WESTERN ROOTS

The Nicholas Earp family moved from Iowa to Temescal, California, in 1878, then to Colton, near San Bernardino, the following year. The following advertisement and paragraph appeared in the Colton Semi-Tropic of November 27, 1880.

GEM SALOON, N. P. EARP, PROPRIETOR, Keeps on hand the best Whiskey, Wines, Brandies, Gin, Rum, Porter, Beer and cigars. Fancy Cocktails, Tom and Jerry, at all times whenever called for.

Call on N. P. Earp and test his superb Tom & Jerry. He is always on hand and ready to wait on customers.

*   *   *

Over the years there have been many claims about Morgan's whereabouts before he arrived in Tombstone in 1880. Recent finds in Montana establish that he was a policeman in the mining town of Butte, beginning December 16, 1889. The following is notice of his resignation; Butte City Council Minutes, March 10, 1880, Butte-Silver Bow Public Archives.

On Reports of officers being called for by His Honor the Mayor, Marshal Warfield presented the names of Thomas Hess and Duncan Gillis to be policemen instead of Morgan Earp and Cal Tolman resigned. Moved and seconded that Thomas Hess and Duncan Gillis be and is hereby appointed by the Council policemen in and for the City of Butte, to fill the vacancies caused by the resignations of Earp and Tolman.

SISTER DESCRIBES BROTHERS

Adelia Earp Edwards in her memoirs recounts some physical and personality descriptions of her brothers.

Wyatt and Virgil were not too much alike in nature. Wyatt and Jim were more alike, and Morg and Warren were too. Virgil was Virgil and there wasn't nobody much like him. He was a fine man. He was the biggest and had a big booming voice and laugh and a real big heart too. You would really have to push him some to make him angry but then he really did explode. I guess Wyatt and Jim were the same that way, like mother too, and me, I reckon. Morg and Warren were like my father more, they were quicker tempered boys. Only Newton and Warren were dark like my father, the other boys favored my mother and were fair.

*　　*　　*

Contrary to popular belief and most prose, Tombstone was a mining center, not a cowboy playground. The place was founded and thrived on silver. The silver was discovered by Ed Schieffelin in 1877, and named "Tombstone" by him in jest, as soldiers claimed that was all he would find there. The following, from Arizona Quarterly Illustrated, of July, 1880, indicates the mining ethos of this community, so young when the Earps arrived on the scene.

As the mines began to attract attention, a town was started on the grounds of the West Side mine, one of the properties of the Tough Nut Co. Soon after, another town called Richmond was started near the Lucky Cuss mine. Both of these were soon found not to contain eligible ground enough for the purposes of the

38

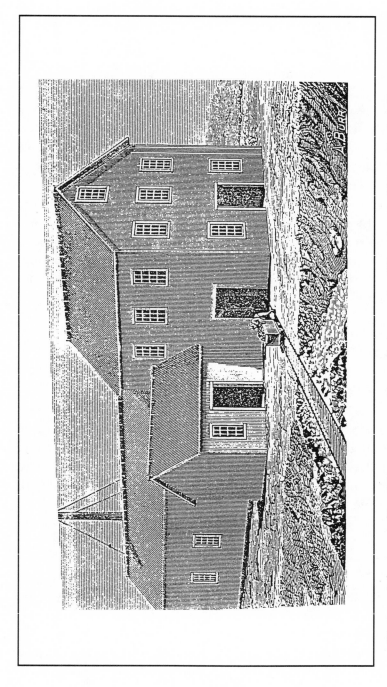

First and foremost, Tombstone was a silver mining and milling town. This is the hoisting works at Contention Mill. Arizona Quarterly Illustrated, April, 1881

camp, as both were upon narrow ridges, with arroyas on each side.

On the fifth day of March 1879, a town site association was formed by Gov. A. P. K. Safford, Judge T. J. Bidwell, A. J. Palmer, W. S. Clark and C. H. Calhoun, who laid out the present site of Tombstone on a wide and level mesa of land, across the arroya from the Tough Nut mine. . . .

The first house in the town was erected by J. B. Allen, on the corner of Fourth and Allen streets, which he occupied as a store. This was erected in June, 1879, and about the same time Charles Brown erected the first installment of his hotel, and Thomas Corrigan started a saloon, now the splendid Alhambra.

*   *   *

EARLY TOMBSTONE AND THE EARPS

Arizona Miner, March 26, 1880.

Deputy U. S. Marshal V. W. Earp arrested a man by the name of C. S. Hogan at Tombstone, a few days since, for counterfeiting trade dollars. He was examined, held to bail in $5,000, but escaped from the Tombstone prison. The plates and dies were found with the prisoner.

*   *   *

U. S. Census, 1880, Tombstone (Pima County), Arizona Territory.

Earp, Alvira [Allie]   22   Nebraska   Keeping House

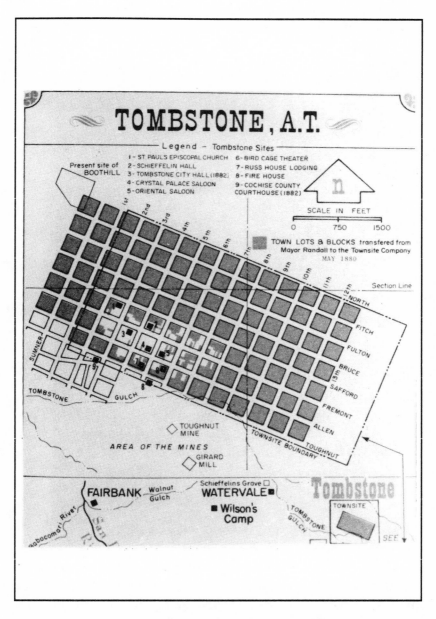

Main streets and buildings of historic Tombstone, when that mining community was in full swing. Don Bufkin Map, Arizona & the West, Spring, 1979

[Virgil's wife]
Earp, Bessie   36   Mo.   Keeping House
  [wife of James]
Earp, Hattie B.   16   Iowa   At Home
  [dau. of James]
Earp, James Cooksey   39   Kentucky   Saloonkeeper
Earp, Mattie   22   Wisconsin   Keeping House
  [common-law wife, Wyatt]
Earp, Virgil Walter   36   Kentucky   Farmer
Earp, Wyatt Berry Stapp   32   Illinois   Farmer

*   *   *

Tombstone Nugget, June 3, 1880.

Among the mines recorded on Monday last, we find the following from this district: Leigh, Nathan Leigh; Evening Star, John Hogan; Mountain Chief, L. Brown; Mineral Hill and Crown Princess, L. Brown and John Hogan; Long Branch, Wyatt Earp; Neberiskie, Turquoise district, F. L. Hebeson and Andrew Nelson; You Bet, E. S. Keeler and Ed. Lyons.

*   *   *

Tombstone Epitaph, November 6, 1880.

Messrs. Earp and Neff received from A. H. Emanuel a few days since the sum of $3000, being the proceeds of sale of the Comstock mine. They have also bonded to the same party the Grasshopper, an extension of the Comstock, for $3000, the bond to run until December 7.

* * *

Virgil arrived in Tombstone wearing a Deputy U. S. Marshal's badge. Wyatt soon received a law enforcement appointment; from Pima County Recorder's Office, Tucson.

Know all Men by these presents that I Charles A. Shibell Sheriff of the County of Pima Territory of Arizona do hereby appoint Wyatt S. Earp of the town of Tombstone in Said County a Deputy Sheriff in and for Said Pima County.

In witness whereof I have hereunto Set My hand this 27th day of July 1880.

/S/ Charles A. Shibell
Sheriff Pima Co. A. T.

* * *

THE WELLS FARGO LINK

Tombstone Epitaph, July 29, 1880.

The appointment of Wyatt Earp as Deputy Sheriff, by Sheriff Shibell, is an eminently proper one, and we, in common with the citizens generally, congratulate the latter on his selection. Wyatt has filled various positions in which bravery and determination were requisites, and in every instance proved himself the right man in the right place. He is at present filling the position of shotgun messenger for Wells, Fargo & Co., which he will resign to accept the later appointment.

Same issue.

James Earp. Arizona Historical Society

Morgan Earp. Arizona Historical Society

Virgil Earp. Arizona Historical Society

Wyatt Earp. Arizona Historical Society

Morgan Earp succeeds his brother as shotgun messenger for Wells, Fargo & Co.

*   *   *

Fred Dodge was sent to Tombstone acting as an undercover agent for the Wells, Fargo office in San Francisco. He became a staunch backer of the Earps, and was particularly intimate with Morgan. The following, from Dodge's Under Cover for Wells, Fargo explains how the first Dodge-Earp encounter on the streets of Tombstone occurred.

When the Stage pulled up, there were many there. I was sitting on the front Dickey right behind the Driver. I always felt "hunches" and I could feel that there was some one looking intently at me. I carefully looked around and I saw two men who were carefully sizeing me up—It was plain to be seen that they were Brothers and that they were outstanding *Men*. There was no one to meet me, and as far as I knew, no one there Knew me. I got down from the Stage like the rest of the Passengers and was standing there, when these 2 men started towards me—I could plainly see that there was nothing wrong in their movements. One of them stepped up to me and put out his hand and said, "My Name is Wyatt Earp," and I said, "My name is Fred Dodge."

We shook hands and he then introduced to me his brother, Virgil Earp—and said, "I suppose that you noticed that we were both looking at you very carefully," and I told him that I had noticed them. So they told me that they were expecting another Brother on any Stage and that He and I looked enough alike to be twins. And as we three moved off a little, we heard several say,

"There is another one of the Earp Boys." Our friendship Commenced right then.

The next day, I think, this other Brother Come—Morgan Earp—and before he got off of the Stage, I could see there was a strong resemblance to Each other. We become very close friends. Morg would sometimes be called Fred and likewise I would be called Morg—this of course was not from our closer friends and associates.

*   *   *

Fred Dodge, in Under Cover for Wells, Fargo explains how the Earps first got connected with that express firm.

I had written to Mr. Valentine [general manager, at San Francisco office] in Answer to a request from him for me to select someone to look after Wells Fargo and Co.'s interest—Run Shot Gun Messenger and Guard heavy shipments of Bullion and Money. I recommended Wyatt Earp, giving what I knew at that time of his past record, and advising Mr. Valentine that with this appointment, the company would receive the Cooperation of all the Brothers. Jim Hume Shortly come there and Made the Arrangements with Wyatt Earp—Wyatt did not know anything at that time about any connection that I had had in this appointment. That my judgment was good in the Selection was proven in many ways by future Events. This also made it more serious regarding myself, as Undercover Man. *I must be undercover* and I can assure you that it required all my resources to remain so.

*   *   *

Wyatt would spend many an evening in the Oriental

49

Saloon, where he not only worked the tables, but for a time had a financial interest. The following is from Clara Brown, columnist for the San Diego Union, issue of August 10, 1880.

Saloon openings are all the rage. The "Oriental" is simply gorgeous and is pronounced the finest place of the kind this side of San Francisco. The bar is a marvel of beauty; the sideboards were made for the Baldwin Hotel; the gaming room connected is carpeted with Brussels, brilliantly lighted, and furnished with reading matter and writing materials for its patrons. Every evening music from a piano and violin attracts a crowd; and the scene is really a gay one—but all for the men.

*   *   *

Extracts and excerpts, Corporate Archives, Wells, Fargo & Co., San Francisco.

GENERAL CASH BOOK

August 1880, salary, Tombstone Wyatt Earp	$125.00
	95.82
September 1880 Tombstone Morgan Earp	45.83
October 1880 Tombstone Morgan Earp	125.00
November 1880 Tombstone Morgan Earp	125.00
December 1880 Tombstone Morgan Earp	125.00
January 1881 Tombstone Morgan Earp	125.00
February 1881 Tombstone Morgan Earp Messenger	95.00

General Cash Book, June 1881 Loss & Damage: Tombstone, Expenses in search of robbers:

V. Earp	32.00
Wy. Earp	72.00
M. Earp	72.00

General Cash Book, October 1881, Loss & Damage: Tombstone,

Expenses in prosecuting robbers of Bisbee Stage. For services in pursuing robbers:

Wyatt Earp	12.00
M Earp	12.00
F Dodge	12.00
Reward Posters	4.00

*   *   *

AS SOLID CITIZENS OF TOMBSTONE

Tombstone Epitaph, August 4, 1880.

Diego Meindies was arrested by Officer [Wyatt] Earp yesterday afternoon on a complaint, charging him with brutally beating a Mexican woman, with whom he had been living. He was placed under bonds of $50 to await his examination before Judge Gray this morning at 9 o'clock.

*   *   *

Tombstone Nugget, August 5, 1880.

A TRICK THAT WAS VAIN Sunday last, a few minutes before the stage was ready to start to Tucson and by which Deputy Sheriff Earp intended to take Roger King into Tucson for lodgment in jail,

51

he was approached by one J. J. Pace, who presented the following order:

BABCOCK: You will please deliver prisoner to J. J.
Pace.   /S/ C. SHABELL

The prisoner being in the hands of Earp instead of Babcock, who is also a deputy, the order was presented to the former, who believed from the general style and incorrect signature that it was a forgery. Babcock believed it to be genuine and advised the delivery of the prisoner to Pace. Thereupon Earp telegraphed to Sheriff Shibell at Tucson in regard to it and received a reply to the effect that the order was a forgery and instructing him to arrest Pace. This was accordingly done. He was brought before Justice Gray Tuesday afternoon, but waived examination and was committed to $500 bonds to appear before the next grand jury.

*   *   *

Tombstone Nugget, August 5, 1880.

Messrs. A. S. Neff and Wyatt S. Earp have bonded the claims known as the Comstock and Grasshopper to R. F. Pixley, of San Francisco, for the sum of $6,000, ten per cent of the amount being paid as a bonus. These properties lie about one-third of a mile north from town and are very promising.

*   *   *

The following is of interest because it shows that Pima County Deputy Sheriff Wyatt Earp, chasing some horse thieves, deputized his brother Morgan, and also brother Virgil, who was already a Deputy U. S. Marshal. From Tombstone Epitaph, August 17, 1880.

Charles Shibell, Sheriff of Pima County, appointed Wyatt as his Deputy in 1880. Arizona Historical Society

On Sunday last Deputy Sheriff Watt Earp received word that five head of horses had been stolen from Mr. Mason, store keeper at Contention City. He immediately dispatched Messrs. Virgil and Morgan Earp in search of the property and thieves. They returned this morning, and inform us that they got on track of the thieves and followed it as far as Charleston, where they heard that the parties for whom they were hunting had at least forty miles the start of them, with twelve horses, and were heading straight for Sonora. They, of course, gave up on the search as useless.

While in Charleston, however, they met Deputy Sheriff Scow, from Camp Grant, who had just arrested a negro in town for the theft of some horses and mules at Camp Grant, in May last. The darkey himself was also in search of a mule that had been stolen from him by a Mexican. Getting a description, the officers started after the Mexican, whom they soon found. He showed fight, but gave up when a six-shooter was run under his nose by Morgan Earp. He was turned over to the Deputy Sheriff at Charleston, and his trial was going on when our informant left. Deputy Sheriff Scow and Officer Miller brought the negro to Tombstone, from whence he will be taken to Camp Grant to-day.

*　　*　　*

Tombstone Epitaph, August 5, 1880.

SHOOTING OF CAPTAIN MALCOLM. About 7 o'clock last evening Chas Bartholomew brought the news to town that Captain Malcolm, an old and well known citizen, living at Waterville, had been killed by a teamster. Deputy Sheriff Earp, accompanied by his brother Morgan, immediately started for the scene of the tragedy. We could not get any of the particulars save that Jose Kelsey was on the track of the teamster.

54

*   *   *

Tombstone Epitaph, September 10, 1880.

TOMBSTONE HOSE COMPANY NO. 1. At a meeting of citizens, held at Kelly's Wine Rooms last evening, Tombstone Hose Company No. 1 was organized, with sixteen members enrolled. H. B. Jones was elected President and Wyatt Earp, Secretary.

*   *   *

Tombstone Epitaph, October 5, 1880.

A WIFE BEATER James Henry was arrested yesterday by Deputy Sheriff Earp on the complaint of his wife, who accused him of beating her. Upon being brought before Judge Gray he was fined $7.50 and bound over to keep the peace in the sum of $200.

*   *   *

More typical work for Wyatt, from Justice Court, Precinct 17, Tombstone, Cochise County Records. W. Shilliam plaintiff, J. B. Stephenson, defendant.

1880, October 8th. On this day W. J. Hunsaker, Esq. appeared before me and plea complaint herein Summons thereon issued returnable October 15th, 1880. Thereon the said attorney presented affidavit for attachment and undertaking on same, both filed and attachment issued.

1880, October 15th. At 10 a. m. today Deputy Sheriff Earp returned Summons personnly served in this County and also returned attachment and reported property attached. And thereon plaintiff by his attorney W. J. Hunsaker moved for default. Defendant failing to appear the court waited for said defendant till after 11 o.c. a.m. and said defendant still failing to appear default is hereby entered. And Judgement is entered on the copy of the bill in the case filed showing that defendant is indebted to plaintiff in the sum of $94.57. It is therefore ordered and adjudged that plaintiff have and recover of said defendant $94.57 and five per cent thereon, $4.12, total $99.29 besides his lawfull disbursement in this case . . . .

    Sheriff's fees $29.00   /S/ James Reilly J. P.

*   *   *

Pete Spence (or Spencer) would figure later in several Earp brothers encounters. This little-known incident establishes that Pete was well known to the family; Tombstone Epitaph, October 24, 1880.

GRAND LARCENY. Pete Spencer was arrested yesterday by Deputy Sheriff Earp on a warrant from Justice Burnett's court, Charleston, charging him with grand larceny. Upon being taken before Judge Burnett he was bound over in the sum of $200 to appear before the next Grand Jury. Bonds were promptly furnished by John Roberts and a party, name unknown. The singular part of the proceeding is that Spence was bound over not on the charge preferred against him, but as a witness. It seems that on the 28th of last month a party in Sonora lost a pair of mules. Shortly after a Mexican sold the mules in Tombstone to Spence and he disposed of them to some other party. The man who lost the mules recognized them in the possession of the party to whom Spence had sold them, and immediately made this charge, stated above, against Spence.

56

*　　*　　*

In later years, ex-Tombstone mayor John Clum recorded his impressions of Wyatt; Clum Papers, University of Arizona Library.

A commanding personality, above six feet in height, well proportioned and neat in his attire. His manner, though friendly, suggested a quiet reserve. His facial features were strong, positive and pleasing. His habitual expression was serious, with a gracious smile when the occasion warranted it—but his mirth was never boisterous (as my own was apt to be). In fact, about the time I was elected mayor of Tombstone, Wyatt was quite my ideal of the strong, manly, serious and capable peace officer—equally unperturbed whether he was anticipating a meeting with a friend or a foe.

*　　*　　*

Virgil Earp, already a Deputy U. S. Marshal, would become famous as Tombstone's chief of police. Before he received that appointment, though, he was scurrying for more humble work; from Tombstone Epitaph, October 28, 1880.

Attention is called to the announcement of V. W. Earp for Constable of the Seventeenth Precinct. Mr. Earp promises all the qualifications necessary for the position, and if elected will no doubt fill the office satisfactorily.

*　　*　　*

Tombstone Epitaph, October 29, 1880, both articles.

TEMPORARY MARSHAL. Virgil Earp was yesterday appointed Marshal by the Town Council, pending the illness of Marshal White. Earp immediately entered upon the discharge of his duty.

ACTING BY AUTHORITY. Some dissatisfaction was manifested this morning at the action of Deputy Sheriff [Wyatt] Earp in releasing one of the parties arrested for implication in the row the previous night. The following note explains itself, and is a complete answer to the unwarranted comments on the officer's action:

TOMBSTONE, October 28, 1880.

WYATT EARP, DEPUTY SHERIFF: Release J. Atkinson immediately, as bail has been given for his appearance. M. GRAY, J. P.

*   *   *

Tombstone Epitaph, October 31, 1880.

WITHDRAWS. In to-days issue will be found the withdrawal of Virgil Earp as candidate for Constable, he having been appointed Marshal. He considers that his time will be fully occupied in the duties incident to that position.

*   *   *

Wyatt had roughed up Curly Bill Brocious during the incident when City Marshal Fred White had been accidentally killed. Wyatt later told editor John Clum the following, which further embittered Brocious; Tombstone Epitaph, October 31, 1880.

"Curly Bill" Brocious, one of the cowboys who fell from the face of the earth during Wyatt's vendetta. Arizona Historical Society

AN OLD OFFENDER. From Deputy Sheriff Earp we learn that the man who killed Marshal White is an old offender against the law. Within the past few years he stopped a stage in El Paso County, Texas, killing one man and dangerously wounding another. He was tried and sentenced to ten years in the penitentiary, but managed to make his escape shortly after being incarcerated. The fact leaked out in this way; On the road to Tucson, Byocins [Brocious] asked Earp where he could get a good lawyer. Earp suggested that Hereford & Zabriskie were considered a good firm. Broscins said that he didn't want Zabriskie, as he had prosecuted him once in Texas. Inquiry on the part of Earp developed the above state of facts.

* * *

Tombstone Epitaph, November 6, 1880.

CLAIM SOLD AND ANOTHER BONDED. Messrs. Earp and Neff received from A. H. Emanuel a few days since the sum of $3000, being the proceeds of sale of the Comstock mine. They have also bonded to the same party the Grasshopper, an extension of the Comstock, for $3000, the bond to run until December 7.

* * *

Tombstone Epitaph, May 8, 1881.

The Earp Brothers and R. J. Winders have applied for a patent for the North Extension of the Mountain Maid, which will appear in the EPITAPH in a few days.

* * *

One of the commonplace but mistaken statements about the factions in Tombstone is that Johnny Behan, Sheriff of the newly formed Cochise County, represented the "old-timers" in the area, and that the Earps and their crowd were new-comers, interlopers. This is far from reality. Deputy U. S. Marshal Virgil Earp arrived in Tombstone in late November, 1879. The following is the first notice of Behan on the scene.

Tombstone Epitaph, September 15, 1880.

Mr. J. H. Behan, ex-Sheriff of Yavapai County, and a member of the last Legislature from Mohave County, accompanied by his son, are guests at the Grand.

* * *

FEUD WITH CURLY BILL

The shooting death of City Marshal Fred White on October 27, 1880, was a pivotal episode for the career of the Earp brothers in Tombstone. William Brocious, "Curly Bill," did the deed, and such was clarified by Wyatt Earp. The following is from Wyatt's testimony in Tucson, as printed in the Arizona Weekly Citizen of January 1, 1881. A permanent grudge—and Curly Bill's death—were results of this incident.

On the 27th of last October was Deputy Sheriff; resided at Tombstone; saw defendant that night at the time Marshal White was shot; was present at the time the fatal shot fired; saw Mr. Johnson there at that time; my brother came up immediately after;

61

this affair occurred back of a building in a vacant lot between Allen and Tough Nut streets; I was in Billy Owen's saloon and heard three or four shots fired; upon hearing the first shot I ran out in the street and I saw the flash of a pistol up the street about a block from where I was; several shots were fired in quick succession; ran up as quick as I could, and when I got there I met my brother, Morgan Earp, and a man by the name of Dodge; I asked my brother who it was that did that shooting; he said he didn't know—some fellows who ran behind that building; I asked him for his six shooter and he sent me to Dodge; after I got the pistol, I run around the building, and as I turned the corner I ran past this man Johnson, who was standing near the corner of the building; I ran between him and the corner of the building, but before I got there I heard White say; "I am an officer; give me your pistol;" and just as I was almost there I saw the defendant pull his pistol out of his scabbard and Marshal White grabbed hold of the barrel of it; the parties were no more two feet apart facing each other; both had hold of the pistol, and just then I threw my arms around the defendant, to see if he had any other weapons, and looked over his shoulder, and White saw me and said; "now, you G____ d_____ s____ of a b_____, give up that pistol;" and he gave a quick jerk and the pistol went off; White had it in his hand, and when he fell to the ground, shot, the pistol dropped and I picked it up; as he fell, he said, "I am shot." The defendant stood still from the time I first saw him until the pistol went off; when I took the defendant in charge he said, "What have I done? I have not done anything to be arrested for." When the pistol exploded I knocked defendant down with my six-shooter; he did not get up until I stepped over and picked up the pistol, which had fallen out of White's hand as he fell I then walked up to defendant, caught him by the collar and told him to get up. I did not notice that he was drunk; if he was I did not notice it.

* * *

PACE QUICKENS, PLOT THICKENS

The Earp plans for a takeover of the **Chief of Police** office following White's death were **dashed by the voters;** from Tombstone Epitaph, November 13, 1880.

THE ELECTION YESTERDAY. The election **for City Marshal,** to fill the vacancy caused by the death of **Fred White, excited** considerable interest and resulted in the **selection of Ben Sippy by** the following vote: Sippy, 311; V. W. Earp, 259; **Sippy's majority,** 52. Mr. Sippy will make an efficient Marshal, **and should receive** the support and assistance of all good citizens.

* * *

Pima County Deputy Sheriff Wyatt Earp was in a dilemma in late 1880. He had received his appointment from Sheriff Shibell, but running against Shibell in the election was Bob Paul, a Western lawman with whom Wyatt was friendly. Wyatt decided to step aside and avoid showing preference; from Pima County Recorder's Office.

Tucson AT November 9th 1880
Charles A. Shibell
Sheriff Pima, Tucson AT
Sir
I have the honor hereunto to resign the office of Deputy Sheriff of Pima County.
Respectfully

/S/ Wyatt S. Earp

*   *   *

Curly Bill was exonerated in the death of City Marshal Fred White, by White himself, in his dying words. This tragedy did not diminish Curly Bill's interest in hell-raising. The following diary entry of January 10, 1881, is from the pen of George W. Parsons; Chafin (ed.), Parsons Diaries.

Cold now nights. Bright, clear, grand weather these days. Fine climate—best I've yet struck. Some more bullying by the cowboys. "Curly Bill" and others captured Charleston the other night and played the devil generally, breaking up a religious meeting by chasing the minister out of the house, putting out lights with pistol balls and going through the town. I think it was tonight they captured the Alhambra Saloon here and raced through the town firing pistols.

*   *   *

In the following instance, Virgil was in his capacity as Deputy U. S. Marshal, and he had deputized Morgan. The quarry was Paullin, a French merchant of Tombstone accused of embezzling. Marshal Earp for some weeks had Paullin under guard in the Earp home, and got to know him quite well, all of which led to some laughs on the Arizona-Mexican border; Tombstone Epitaph, March 11, 1881.

Virgil and Morgan Earp are on the track of Paullin, somewhere in the Sulphur Spring Valley, and the chances are that they will catch him.

*   *   *

Tombstone Epitaph, April 8, 1881.

Readers of the EPITAPH will remember an item which appeared in these columns a few days since, announcing that Paullin had been recaptured in Hermosillo by Deputy United States Marshal Burke, of Willcox. Burke had gone to Sonora to hunt for Collins, alias "Shotgun," the Willcox murderer. In Hermosillo he struck a whole bevy of fugitives, consisting of Paullin, Collins, and "Red," the Silver city horse-thief who escaped from the Tombstone dry-goods box a short time ago. Paullin is an adept in the ways that are dark and tricks that are vain, and shortly after his arrest he wrote a long and very friendly letter to Deputy United States Marshal, Virgil W. Earp, of this city, stating that he was very sorry he had been obliged to leave Tombstone without bidding the Earp boys goodbye, and asking Virgil to forward his clothes, books, papers, etc. to Hermosillo. This cheeky effusion he in some manner caused to fall under Burke's eye, and that guileless and trusting official evidently thought that Virg would hardly thank him for bringing back to captivity such a dear friend as Paullin must be. So he let Paullin meander peacefully away, and his stupidity will no doubt prove very cheering to the wily Frenchman as he betakes himself to pastures new.

* * *

The comings and goings of the Earps were well chronicled by both Tombstone newspapers. James ran a saloon in town. The following note appeared in the Epitaph of May 6, 1881.

MR. J. C. EARP and wife left for Colton, California, last evening. He expects to be absent a month or six weeks.

* * *

While Virgil, Wyatt, Morgan, and James Earp were earning a living as lawmen, shotgun riders, and saloon operators, one of their Caliornia cousins was an established farmer, and a fervent teetotaler. This is from the Colusa County, California history of 1880.

Peter A. Earp, born September 12, 1835, in Kentucky. Parents' names, Lorenzo D. and Nancy Earp. Until he was twenty-one years of age he stayed with his father who was a farmer. In 1846 he came to Illinois, to Iowa in 1853, to California in 1859, from Iowa, by land. The trip occupied four months and was quite pleasant; no trouble with Indians, and no sickness or death in the train. . . . He mined on Yuba river one month in 1859, but was not very successful, so he abandoned mining and went to Sutter county, where he remained until 1863. Has lived in the valley, and has resided ever since within fifteen miles of where he now resides, near Sycamore, on Grand Island.

Mr. Earp came to this county October 1862, engaged in farming and stock-raising on one hundred and sixty acres of rich river land, adapted to wheat, fruit, broom corn and vegetables which grow in this climate. He has ten horses, ten head of cattle, fifty hogs, one hundred sheep; keeps stock enough for home use.

Married Miss Martha Helton in 1863. She is a native of Missouri, but was brought up in California. They have seven children, four sons and three daughters. Mr. Earp is an earnest and conscientious temperance advocate, and has done much to advance the cause.

The name Earp in this era was not necessarily a synonym for wanderer or saloon keeper. The Earp boys' cousin, Peter A. Earp, was a solid citizen-rancher and teetotaler in California. Colusa County, California History, 1880

* * *

VIRGIL TAKES OVER

John Clum, ex-Indian Agent and newly elected Mayor of Tombstone, explains his relationships with the Earps and how Virgil came to be Chief of Police; from Arizona Historical Review, II, October, 1929.

It was about midnight when I rolled into Tombstone on the stage from Benson. This was our first big fire—and a disastrous one. The following day I learned that during my absence Ben Sippy, the city marshal, had decamped—leaving the city without a police head; that Virgil Earp, with the approval of the city councilmen, had assumed that responsibility in the emergency and that he had rendered a most efficient and satisfactory service. The result was that Virgil was retained as Chief of Police until he was so seriously wounded on the night of Dec. 28, 1881.

Thus it will appear that for six months during my administration as mayor of Tombstone, Virgil Earp held the position of Chief of Police. Obviously, I came to know him well—and liked him very much. He was a courageous and efficient officer. Once he arrested me for fast riding.

I was a resident of Tombstone all of the time the Earp brothers were there. I knew Virgil and Wyatt and Morgan and Jimmy. They all had the reputation of being handy and effective with a six-shooter, but I always regarded them as law-abiding and orderly citizens—and I was not a "tenderfoot." I came to New Mexico ten years before—in 1871—at the age of twenty. On that trip I saw the buffalo and picturesque buffalo hunters in broad hats and buckskins. From August, 1874, until July 1877, I was in charge of the

John Clum, Mayor of Tombstone and editor of the Epitaph.
Arizona Quarterly Illustrated, January 1881

Apache Indians. I had been active on the frontier and knew something of the character of its citizens.

* * *

Clum's mention of Virgil's service during the 1881 fire was expanded in this notice from the Tombstone Epitaph, which was reprinted on p. 323 of The Private Journal of George Whitwell Parsons.

With the dawn of Thursday's sun, men, women and children were astir, looking about to see what had been left them out of the ruins wrought the evening before. There was little but desolation, the few goods they had saved being badly damaged. Nothing dismayed, the business portion of the community set about them to make ready for the new stocks that had been ordered by telegraph the night before-figuratively speaking, the dispatches being written by the light of their burning goods. The unsettled title to lots led to some disturbance between the lessees and lessors, but thanks to the prompt and decisive action of Marshal Earp there was no damage done. After consultation with the Mayor and councilmen, and being told to use his own judgment in the matter, he appeared upon the scene of action and told the contestants that he should use his authority and the full power of the police force to maintain the same order of things that existed before the fire, and up to such time as the courts settle the question of titles. This decisive and just action on the part of the Marshal acted like oil upon troubled waters, and peace and order were restored. This action of Marshal Earp cannot be too highly praised, for in all probability it saved much bad blood and possibly bloodshed.

From Arizona Quarterly Illustrated, *July, 1880*

*   *   *

Minutes, Tombstone Common Council, June 6, 1881, in Arizona Historical Society, Tucson.

On motion, Chief of Police Sippy was granted two weeks leave of absence...On motion, Virgil Earp was appointed Chief of Police during absence of Sippy and instructed to file bonds in the sum of $5000.00.

*   *   *

The Medigovitch Collection, Arizona Historical Society, contains Tombstone records during Virgil's tenure as Chief of Police. Following is a typical monthly report filed by Virgil.

71

To the Honorable the Mayor and Common Council of the City of Tombstone Arizona

Gentlemen

The following is the report of the Chief of Police for the month of June 1881 commencing June 7th and ending June 30th 1881.

Received of Benj Sippy two pair nippers;, one pair handcuffs; one water bucket; one tin cup; two slop buckets; two pair Blankets. .Number of Officers on duty five (5). Names of Officers, A. Carrillo; T. Cornelison, G. W. Chapman, George Mayee; George Bridge.

Names of Officers now on duty, A. G. Boone, George Myer, George Bridger, Al Young; James Flynn, G. W. Chapman. Officer A. Carrillo resigned June 20th 1881. A. S. Bronk appointed Special Policeman June 20th 1881 via Carrillo resigned; Officer Thomas Cornelison reported Sick, June 13th 1881 and Before he reported for duty was arrested for Grand Larceny and Sent to County Jail. Al Young was appointed in Cornelison place June 132 1881. James Flynn was appointed Special Policeman June 22nd 1881.

Number of arrests during the Month viz:

Petit Larceny	3
D. D. [drunk & disorderly]	18
Assault with D. W.	2
& Bat.	2
Fighting & D. the P.[Dist. the Peace]	14
Against O. No. 10	2
C. C. W. [carrying concealed weapons]	3
Resisting Officer	1
Grand Larceny	1
Fast Driving	1
Drawing Deadly W	1
TOTAL	48

POLICE DEPARTMENT.
CITY OF TOMBSTONE.

V. W. EARP,
CHIEF OF POLICE.

TOMBSTONE, A. T., July 8th 188 1

City of Tombstone
To George Boridge

To Seven days Work as Policeman

V. W. Earp
Chief of Police

Virgil was the head of law enforcement in Tombstone, and the position was known both as Chief of Police and City Marshal. Arizona Historical Society

73

Arizona Quarterly Illustrated, January 1881

No. of Prisoners Placed in Jail	40
" " Released from Jail	40
Fines Paid	$323.50
" Remitted	39.00
Total imposed	$362.50

/S/ **V. W. Earp**
Chief of Police

(Note: also known as City Marshal)

74

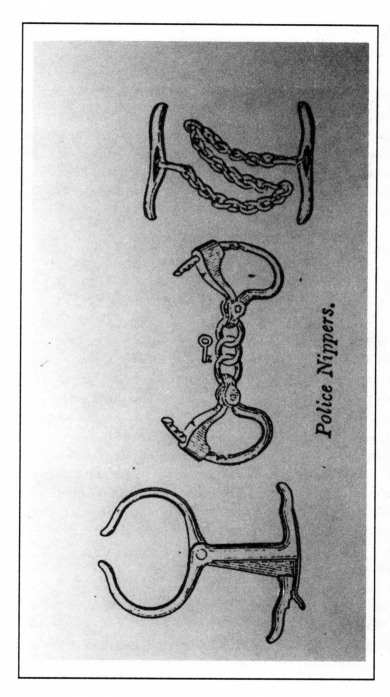

Police Nippers.

"Nippers," mentioned in Virgil's police report, are handcuffs, leg irons, or "come-alongs" used in law enforcement. Knight's American Mechanical Dictionary, 1881

*   *   *

One of Virgil's problems was younger brother Warren, an occasional deputy to Virgil, messenger, etc., ever trying to be like brothers Virgil and Wyatt. The following note appeared in the Tombstone Epitaph of March 22, 1881, and was typical of the press that Warren would generate for decades.

WARREN EARP, for discharging firearms within the city limits, was fined $25 in Recorder Wallace's court yesterday.

*   *   *

In 1924, the famous, wealthy actress Lotta Crabtree died in Boston, apparently without heirs. A claimant, a daughter of her brother, Jack Crabtree, tried unsuccessfully to prove a relationship. Jack had been in Tombstone during the exciting period of 1880-81, and his daughter's attorneys had several well known Tombstone personalities testify to this point. Wyatt testified in court in Los Angeles in 1927, and his comments, although not of great help to the daughter, are fascinating glimpses of life in Tombstone. The following excerpts from Wyatt's testimony are from the Crabtree Case File, Harvard Law School Library.

(Regarding a rooming house.)
Q Did you know the lady who ran that?
A Yes.
Q Who was it?
A Mrs. Falleon. Afterwards she married a man named Taylor.
I met Mrs Crabtree at Mrs Falleon San Jose rooming house on two

Claim No. 8 2

Warren Earp
special police
June 22

4 - 00

Filed. JUL 8 1881

Paid. JUL 8 1881

Warrant, No. 164

Warren was one of the special policemen sworn in by Chief of Police Virgil Earp during the Tombstone fire of July, 1881. Arizona Historical Society

or three occasions. I recollect one occasion very well, where there had been a man shot, by the name of Storms, and he had a room at the San Jose rooming house and we took Storms down there to his room. The doctor was going to hold a post mortem and they wanted me to stick around, and being there I met Mrs Crabtree. She had her baby with her than and I had quite a long talk with her with regard to the shooting and how it came up and what it was about, and all that. On two or three other occasions I met her there. I used to take my prisoners down to the San Jose rooming house. They had no jail in Tombstone at that time. That was before the county was divided. It was all Pima County and we had to take our prisoners to Tucson. In holding them in Tombstone I used to get a room in the San Jose and put a guard over them and in that way I met Mrs Crabtree on two or three occasions.

(Regarding places where Wyatt saw Crabtree's wife)

Q You never saw Mrs Crabtree there again?

A Just once after that.

Q And that is all?

A Yes. I saw her just twice at that House. I met her at other times at an ice cream parlor.

Q What ice cream parlor?

A On Fourth Street between Allen and Fremont.

Q Whose place?

A A woman named Hinckley. She afterwards married a man named Fay, a reporter on the Nugget.

Q What was she doing?

A I don't know. I used to go there pretty often. I liked ice cream and I met her over there. At one time I thought maybe she worked there.

Q Was she behind the counter?

A No, I don't know as they had a counter. They had tables around the room and another room in back.

Prominent stage actress Lotta Crabtree. Wyatt knew her brother Jack in Tombstone and later testified in the celebrated Crabtree estate case. Wells, Fargo History Room, San Francisco

Q Did you ever know what her maiden name was, her first name?

A No.

Q Never heard of it?

A I have heard it since this case came up.

(Wyatt is asked his occupation in Tombstone.)

Q What did you do besides being deputy sheriff and marshal?

A What did I do?

Q Yes.

A Well, I dealt awhile in pasteboard and ivory.

Q Well, you are talking to people who don't know what those things are.

A Dealing faro bank.

Q Where was that?

A In Tombstone.

Q What place?

A That was the Oriental.

Q Was that on the main street?

A On the business street.

Q On Allen Street?

A Yes.

Q Was the Bird Cage open while you were there?

A Yes.

Q Do you remember when that was opened?

A Some time in 1880. I don't recollect just when, just what month. It was about the latter part of 1880.

* * *

GOOD GUYS, BAD GUYS: WHICH IS WHICH?

The alignment of forces in newly-formed Cochise County

has been the subject of bitter dispute to this day; Earps, city folk, miners, leading citizens on one side, Sheriff Behan, most rural population, and the "cowboys" on the other. William Henry Bishop wrote an account of Tombstone in Harper's Monthly for March, 1883, and stands the test of time well. Following are a few excerpts.

From the hygienic point of view, whiskey and cold lead are mentioned as the leading diseases at Tombstone. What with the leisure that seems to prevail, the constant drinking and gambling at the saloons, and the universal practice of carrying deadly weapons, there is but one source of astonishment, and that is that the cold-lead disease should claim so few victims. . . .

A further element, in addition to the silver mines, adds to the exceptional liveliness of Tombstone. It has attained a certain fame already for the doings of its "Cow-boys." The term cow-boys was at first applied to persons engaged in the cattle business indiscriminately, but while still including the honest sort, has been narrowed down so as to mean particularly a class who have become stealers of cattle, at first over the Mexican frontier, then at home, and terrorists generally in their day and generation. Exceptional desperadoes of this class, such as "Billy the Kid," "Curly Bill," and "Russian George," have been scourges of whole districts in Colorado, New Mexico, and Arizona. . . .The cow-boys frequenting Tombstone at this time were generally from ranches in the San Pedro and San Simon valleys. There were said to be strongholds in the San Simon Valley for concealing stolen cattle, until rebranded and prepared for market, where no officer of the law ever ventured. . . .

Our visit happened to be timed upon the heels of a conflict making the most tragic page yet written in the annals of Tombstone. Official opinions were evenly divided about it, the sheriff

81

extending his sympathy to one party, the city marshal, who was, in fact, its leader, to the other. City Marshal Earp, with his two brothers, and one "Doc" Holliday, a gambler, came down the street armed with rifles and opened fire on the two Clanton brothers and the two McLowry brothers.

*   *   *

The situation among the Tombstone factions is high-lighted by these comments from Fred Dodge, in Under Cover for Wells, Fargo.

Dayly the situation become more intense. Morgan Earp and I were still living in the Cabbin on the lot that the Bird Cage Theater was later built. Wyatt was with us most of the time, but he was desirous that we give up living there for the reasons that we were too much exposed to assassination. And I feel sure that that was the main reason that Wyatt Stayed with us so much.

*   *   *

The "cowboy" faction was not just wild, they were law-breakers, just as the Harper's correspondent had con-cluded. The Clanton family were leaders in this group. Shortly before the famous Tombstone shootout, the leader of the Clanton group "bought the farm" in bizarre circum-stances. The following diary entry by George Parsons of August 17, 1881, stands the test of time regarding the last hours of Newman "Old Man" Clanton; Chafin (ed.), Parsons Diaries.

Bad trouble on the border and this time looks more serious

THE SHERIFF OF TOMBSTONE AND HIS CONSTITUENTS.

Bishop, who wrote the Tombstone article for Harper's *referred to the "The Sheriff of Tombstone." Actually, it was Johnny Behan, sheriff of the newly created Cochise County, with Tombstone as county seat.* Harper's Monthly, March, 1883

Johnny Behan, Sheriff of the newly created Cochise County.
Arizona Historical Society

than anything yet. Dick Gray, the lame one, was killed by some Mexicans along with several others, among them the notorious crane [Jim Crane], and revenge seems the order of the day, a gang having started out to make trouble. [Others killed in the Guadulupe Canyon on August 13 included William Lang, Charles Snow, and Newman H. "Old Man" Clanton, father of the Clanton boys.] This killing business by the Mexicans, in my mind, was perfectly justifiable as it was in retaliation for killing of several of them and their robbery by cowboys recently, this same Crane being one of the number. Am glad they killed him. As for the others, if not guilty of cattle stealing, they had no business to be found in such bad company.

*   *   *

TOWARDS DESTINY AND FAME

The Tombstone shootout had many witnesses, but the following report, from Mayor John Clum, was of an event of that morning. Clum, walking down the street in the morning, met Ike Clanton, and witnessed history in the making; from Clum Papers, University of Arizona Library.

"Good morning, Ike," I said, "any new war on today?"

"Nothin' perticular," drawled Ike, turning on his cowboy heel and ambling down Fourth street. That convinced me that Ike had something sinister on his mind, because usually he was more talkative. . .less taciturn. While I was debating what to do in the premises, I saw our chief of police, Virgil Earp, sauntering down the street, toward Ike.

"Hello, Ike," said Virgil, "what are you doing in town?"

"Nothin' perticular," replied Ike.

85

"Why the Winchester?"

"Oh, just happened to have it with me," said Ike, edging away.

"Wait a minute, Ike," said Virgil, taking hold of Ike's arm. "let's you and I go over and call on Judge Wallace. You can tell him why you brought that cannon in town with you." All of which meant, of course, that Ike was arrested. They walked down the street. . .Virgil still holding Ike's arm.

Suddenly Ike made a break. . .tried to wrench away from Virgil's grip. But Virgil was on the job. . .pulled his six-shooter, and cracked Ike over the head with the butt end of it. Ike stretched his length on the sidewalk. Wyatt and Morgan Earp happened along about that time. The Earp brothers had an uncanny habit of happening along when trouble was brewing. Virgil, Wyatt, and Morgan disarmed Ike. . .revived him, and took him to the court, where Judge Wallace fined him $25. . .and retained his weapons. Ike did not like that a bit.

"Wait till I get another gun," he yelled, "I'll kill every damn one of you Earps." Whereupon Morgan Earp pulled his own six-shooter out of its holster. . .and offered it to Ike, handle first. Ike tried to grab it. . .but one of the deputy sheriffs pushed Ike back. . .told Morgan to put his gun away and get out of the court room.

*   *   *

STREET SHOOT-OUT IN TOMBSTONE

The famous shoot-out on the streets of Tombstone on October 27, 1881, is the most famous such episode in the history of the West, and has a literature of its own. Partisan accounts are many, and the incompleteness of the information puzzles and intrigues us to this day. If a reader follows the contemporary accounts of the trial in the Tombstone

Joseph "Ike" Clanton, who probably triggered the animosity that led to the Tombstone shootout, was not a casualty there. Ike was killed by a sheriff's posse in Graham County, Arizona, in 1887. New York Historical Society

Epitaph and Tombstone Nugget, and reads the testimony gathered by Turner in O. K. Corral Inquest, he probably has as good information as can be obtained. The following brief passages, taken from Turner's Inquest, are enough to give the flavor of the day, and the depth of bitterness on both sides.

Joseph "Ike" Clanton, and something of the events of the day prior to the shootout, follow.

The night before the shooting, I went into the Occidental Lunch Room for a lunch, and while there, Doc Holliday came in and commenced abusing me. He had his hand on his pistol and called me a damned son-of-a-bitch, and told me to get my gun out. I told him I did not have any gun. I looked around and I seen Morg Earp sitting at the bar, behind me, with his hand on his gun. Doc Holiday kept on abusing me. I then went out the door.

Virg Earp, Wyatt, and Morg were all out there. Morg Earp told me if I wanted a fight to turn myself loose. They all had their hands on their pistols while they were talking to me. I told them again I was not armed. Doc Holliday said, "You son-of-a-bitch, go arm yourself then!" I did go off and heel myself. I came back and played poker with Virg Earp, Tom McLaury, and other parties until daylight. Virg Earp played poker with his pistol in his lap all the time. At day light he got up and quit the game. We were playing in the Occidental. I followed Virg Earp out when he quit. I told him that I was abused the night before and I was in town. Then he told me he was going to bed.

One of the more objective, useful reports on that fateful day was from railroad engineer B. F. Sills, a stranger in town.

John H. "Doc" Holliday. Arizona Historical Society

I saw four or five men standing in front of the O. K. Corral, talking of some trouble they had had with Virgil Earp, and they made threats at the time, that on meeting him they would kill him on sight. Someone of the party spoke up at the time and said that they would kill the whole party of the Earps when they met them. I then walked up the street and made enquiries to know who Virgil Earp and the Earps were. A man on the street pointed out Virgil Earp to me and told me that he was the city marshal. I went over and called him to one side and told him the threats I had overheard this party make. One of the men has a bandage around his head at the time, and the day of the funeral he was pointed out to me as Isaac Clanton. I recognized him as one of the party.

City Marshal Virgil Earp explains his dealings with Sheriff Johnny Behan.

I called on Johnny Behan who refused to go with me, to go help disarm these parties. He said if he went along with me, there would be a fight sure; that they would not give up their arms to me. He said, "They won't hurt me," and "I will go down alone and see if I can disarm them." I told him that was all I wanted them to do; to lay off their arms while they were in town. Shortly after he left, I was notified that they were on Fremont Street, and I called on Wyatt and Morgan Earp, and Doc Holliday to go and help me disarm the Clantons and McLaurys. We started down Fourth Street to Fremont, turned down Fremont west, towards Fly's lodging house. When we got about somewhere by Bauer's butcher shop, I saw the parties before we got there, in a vacant lot between the photograph gallery and the house west of it. The parties were Ike and Billy Clanton, Tom and Frank McLaury, Johnny Behan, and the Kid.

Johnny Behan seen myself and party coming down towards

90

them. He left the Clanton and McLaury party and came on a fast walk towards us, and once in a while he would look behind at the party he left, as though expecting danger of some kind. He met us somewhere close to the butcher shop. He threw up both hands, like this and said, "For God's sake, don't go there or they will murder you!"

I said, "Johnny, I am going down to disarm them."

Cochise County Sheriff Johnny Behan, a friend to the "cowboys," testifies as to his attempt to disarm the cowboys just before the shootout.

About that time I saw Ike Clanton and Tom McLaury down below Fly's building. I said to Frank McLaury, "Come along with me." We went to where Ike Clanton and Tom McLaury were standing. I said to them, "Boys, you must give up your arms."

When I arrived there, I found Ike Clanton, Tom McLaury, William Clanton, and William Claiborne there. Frank McLaury went along with me. I said to the boys, "you have got to give up your arms." Frank McLaury demurred. He did not seem inclined at first to be disarmed. Ike Clanton told me that he had nothing, that he was not armed. I put my arm around his waist to see if he was. I found that he was not. Tom McLaury showed me by pulling his coat open that he was not armed. I saw five standing there. I asked them how many there were of their party. They said, "Four." Claiborne said he was not one of the party, that he was there wanting them to leave town. I then said, "Boys, you must go up to the Sheriff's Office and lay off your arms, and stay there until I get back." I told them I was going to disarm the other party.

At that time I saw Earps and Holliday coming down the sidewalk on the south side of Fremont Street. They were between the Post Office and Bauer's Butcher Shop. I mean Morgan Earp,

91

Frank McLaury. Arizona Historical Society

Tom McLaury. Arizona Historical Society

Wyatt Earp, Virgil Earp, and Doc Holliday. I said to the Clanton party, "Wait here. I see them coming down. I will go up and stop them." I walked up the street about 22 or 23 steps. I met them at Bauer's Butcher Shop, and told them not to go any further, that I was down there for the purpose of disarming the Clantons and McLaurys. They wouldn't heed me, paid no attention. And I said, "Gentlemen, I am Sheriff of the County, and I am not going to allow any trouble if I can help it." They brushed past me. I turned and went with them. I was probably a step or two in the rear as we went down the street. I was expostulating with them all this time.

Who fired the first shot is a question still being asked, but the testimony seems to place the credit or blame for this on Wyatt. Here is a portion of Wyatt's testimony.

I had my pistol in my overcoat pocket, where I had put it when Behan told us he had disarmed the other parties. When I saw Billy Clanton and Frank McLaury draw their pistols, I drew my pistol. Billy Clanton leveled his pistol at me, but I did not aim at him. I knew that Frank McLaury had the reputation of being a good shot and a dangerous man, and I aimed at Frank McLaury. The first two shots were fired by Billy Clanton and myself, he shooting at me, and I shooting at Frank McLaury. I don't know which was fired first. We fired almost together. The fight then became general.

After about four shots were fired, Ike Clanton ran up and grabbed my left arm. I could see no weapon in his hand, and thought at the time he had none, and so I said to him, "The fight has commenced. Go to fighting or get away." At the same time pushing him off with my left hand, like this. He started and ran down the side of the building and disappeared between the lodging house and photograph gallery.

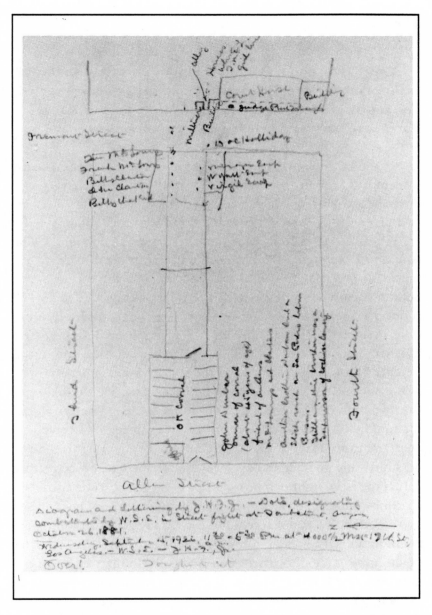

Wyatt's sketch of the shootout, drawn by him in 1926. **Autry Museum of Western Heritage**

There is no good, single account of the actual shootout, as the many versions by participants and bystanders varied. The following few comments, by saloon keeper Robert S. Hatch, are one man's view of the famous event.

As the Earp party got within eight or ten feet of them, I heard someone say, who I thought was Virgil Earp, "We have come down here to disarm you and arrest you!", or words to that effect. In a few seconds after this was said, the shooting commenced.

I turned to Billy Soule [a deputy sheriff] and said to him, "This is none of our fight. We had better get away from here." As I turned to go, I saw Billy Clanton standing near the corner of the building below Fly's house with a pistol in his hand, in the act of shooting. There had probably been three or four shots fired at that time. I immediately ran up the street and went in to Bauer's butcher shop, the Union Market. Probably went in nearly to the butcher block in the back end of the shop, turned and went back to the door on the west side of the building. Saw Doc Holliday and the man who had been pointed out to me as Frank McLaury near the middle of Fremont Street, probably about ten or twelve feet apart. McLaury made a remark like this: "I've got you this time!", or something to that effect. McLaury seemed to be retreating across the street to the opposite side. As he got near the corner of an adobe building on the opposite side of the street, he stopped and stood with a pistol across his arm, in the act of shooting; his pistol in his right hand and resting on his left arm, as if in the act of shooting. At about that time, I saw Doc Holliday and Morgan Earp, who both seemed to be shooting in the direction of Frank McLaury. Frank McLaury fell to the ground about that time, as though he was shot. The shooting seemed to be over about that time.

This version of the shootout is from Turner's The Earps Talk

*   *   *

**Diarist George Parsons was not in Tombstone the day of
the gunfight. His diary entry of October 27 has a few of the
facts confused, but he has the proper measure of the
bitterness; Chafin (ed.), Parsons Diaries.**

At Charleston we dined by invitation of H., and reached
Tombstone about 5 o'clock. Much excitement in town and people
apprehensive and scary. A bad time yesterday when Wyatt, Virgil
and Morgan Earp with Doc Holliday had a street fight with the two
McLowerys and Bill Clanton and Ike, all but the latter being killed,
and W. and M. Earp wounded. Desperate men and a desperate
encounter. Bad blood has been brewing for some time, and I was
not surprised at the outbreak. It is only a wonder it has not
happened before.

*   *   *

JUSTICE CLOUDED

**The conclusion of Justice Wells Spicer is a strong
statement, in considerable detail, which justifies the action
of the Earp party. Virgil and Morgan were recovering from
wounds, so Wyatt and Doc Holliday were questioned. A few
of Spicer's comments follow; from Gary Robert's editing of
the Spicer decision, Montana Magazine of History.**

I also give great weight in this matter to the testimony of
Sheriff Behan, who said that on one occasion, a short time ago,
Isaac Clanton told him that he [Clanton], had been informed that
the sheriff was coming to arrest him, and that he [Clanton] armed

Mining Engineer George Whitwell Parsons, whose journal entries shed so much light on early Tombstone. He was also an amateur actor, which may account for this outlandish outfit. Arizona Historical Society

his crowd with guns and was determined not be arrested by the sheriff, or words to that effect. And Sheriff Behan further testified that a few minutes before the Earps came to them that he, as sheriff, had demanded of the Clantons and McLowrys that they give up their arms, and that they demurred, as he said, and did not do it, and that Frank McLowry refused and gave as a reason that he was not ready to leave town just then, and would not give up his arms unless the Earps were disarmed, that is, that the chief of police and his assistants should be disarmed.

In view of the past history of the county, and the generally believed existance at this time of desperate, reckless men in our midst, banded together for mutual support, and living by felonious and predatory pursuits, regarding neither life or property in the career, and at the same time for men to parade the streets armed with repeating rifles and six-shooters, and demand that the chief of police and his assistants should be disarmed, is a proposition both monstrous and startling. This was said by one of the deceased only a few minutes before the arrival of the Earps.

Another fact that rises up pre-eminent in the consideration of the said affair, is the leading fact that the deceased from the very first inception of the encounter were standing their ground and fighting back, giving and taking death with unflinching bravery. It does not appear to have been a wanton slaughter of unresisting and unarmed innocents, who were yielding, graceful submission to the officers of the law, or surrendering to, or fleeing from their assailants, but armed and defiant men, accepting the wager of battle and succumbing only in death. . . .

I can not resist the conclusion that the defendants were fully justified in committing these homicides; that it was a necessary act, done in the discharge of an official duty. . . .

I conclude the performance of the duty imposed upon me by saying, in the language of the statute, "There being no sufficient

Justice Wells Spicer. Arizona Historical Society

cause to believe the within names" Wyatt S. Earp and John H. Holliday, "Guilty of the offense mention within," I order them to be released.

WELLS SPICER, MAGISTRATE

*   *   *

Fred Dodge a half century after the shootout recalled the atmosphere and situation the night before, when the drinking and name-calling began; Under Cover for Wells, Fargo.

Sometime before midnight, Morgan Earp and I were in the Alhambra—and opposite the Bar in the front part was the Can Can Lunch and Eating Counter Kept by a man named Welsh, Who I Knew in Bodie where he had a place of the same Kind and same name. While Morg and I were sitting in the rear part, Ike Clanton come in and set at the Lunch Counter. It could be seen that he had been Drinking Sufficiently to loosen up his tongue and make him talkative. Soon after, Doc Holliday come in and Seeing Ike, he went over to him and Said, "I hear you are going to Kill me, now is your time to go to work." Ike Clanton said that he did not have any Gun. Doc called him a liar. Doc's vocabulary of profanity and obscene language was monumental and he worked it proficiently in talking to Ike. Morg was going to take me to my room, I was sitting in a Chair and Morg was sitting on the Edge of a Table, when these men Come in. Morg remarked, "This won't do," and stepped over to Doc Holliday and took him by the Arm and led him away to the door where he met Wyatt and Virgil Earp and they took Doc Away.

Morg assisted me to my room and he said that he would go and see what had become of the Boys and Doc—And tell Wyatt about

102

the message that I had received from J. B. Ayers in Charleston [information about stage robbers]. Morg said that this did not look good—but some of the Cow Boys had left town.

*   *   *

First accounts of the famous shootout were so confused that Wyatt's name was not even mentioned; Los Angeles Herald, October 27, 1881.

SHOOTING AFFRAY AT TOMBSTONE-THREE "GOOD" COWBOYS. Tombstone, Oct. 26th.—A sanguinary shooting affray occurred on Fremont street this afternoon. Four cowboys have been in town for a few days past, drinking heavily and making themselves generally obnoxious by their boisterous conduct. This morning city Marshal V. W. Earp, arrested one for disorderly conduct, and he was fined $25, which he paid, and was disarmed. He left the Justice's Court swearing vengeance. The Sheriff, Marshal Earp and his brother Morgan tried to induce the party to leave town, but they were thirsting for gore and refused to be pacified. About 3 p. m. the Earp brothers and J. H. Halliday met the cowboys, who drew upon them at once, when a lively fire commenced from the cowboys against the three citizens. About thirty shots were fired rapidly, and when the smoke of battle cleared away it was found that Jim and Frank McLoury were gasping in the agonies of death. Bill Clanton was mortally wounded and died shortly after. Morgan Earp was wounded in the shoulder, it is thought seriously, V. W. Earp received a flesh wound in the calf of the leg and Halliday escaped unhurt, but with several bullet holes in his clothes. The streets immediately filled with resolute citizens, many of whom were armed with rifles and pistols. There is great excitement but no further trouble is

103

anticipated. Ike Clanton, one of the cowboys, escaped with a slight wound, and is now in jail. The Sheriff's posse are now under arms. Morgan Earp, after he was wounded and had fallen, struggled to his feet and continued the fight till he emptied his revolver. His wound is not thought to be serious. The citizens are determined to put down the riotous element at all hazards.

* * *

For half a century, ex-Tombstone Mayor John Clum told, and wrote, about how close he was to the Earps, how highly he thought of Virgil, and so forth. After the shootout, Clum bowed to community pressure; from Minutes, Tombstone Common Council, entry of October 29, 1881.

Council met pursuant to call of Mayor. Present Messrs. Harwood, Pridham and Tribolet. Absent Gray. Mayor Clum presiding.

Mayor Clum stated that meeting was called to consider grave charges against Chief of Police Earp and it was ordered that pending investigation of said charges Chief Earp be temporarily suspended and James Flynn act as Chief during such suspension.

The matter of appointing special policemen was left at the discretion of the Mayor and Chief of Police.

On motion Council adjourned.

John S. Clum

Mayor

* * *

The pressure on Clum, from a very divided citizenry, is

evident from these paragraphs in the San Diego Union of December 13, 1881.

The Earp trial dragged along for nearly a month, and excited more interest than any trial ever before held in Tombstone. Judge Spicer, with an elaborate recapitulation of the evidence on both sides, gave a verdict acquitting the Earps, on the ground that the homicide was necessary to preserve their own lives.

There being two strong parties in the camp, of course this verdict is satisfactory to but one of them. The other accepts it with a very bad grace, and a smoldering fire exists, which is liable to burst forth at some unexpected moment. If the Earps were not men of great courage, they would hardly dare remain in Tombstone.

*　　*　　*

The following, from the Minutes of the Tombstone Common Council of October 31, 1881, only days after the famous shootout, forces a question—were the assessment changes related to a change in climate?

On Motion, following changes in assessments were made:

Wyatt Earp, personal property $190.00 added.

James, Virgil and Wyatt Earp, 30 acres surface of Mattie Blaylock and Long Branch mines, $2500.00 added.

Virgil, Wyatt and James Earp and A. S. Neff, ten acres surface of Grasshopper Mine, $1000.00 added.

James Earp, 3 lots, block V, $400.00 added.

Winders, R. J., V. W., James and Wyatt Earp, lots 1-2-3-4 block M, reduced from $800.00 to $500.00, lots 1 & 2 block 29 assessed to [?] parties on application.

105

*　　*　　*

The U. S. Marshal of Arizona Territory, Crawley P. Dake, had in 1879 created Virgil a deputy, an office which Dake transferred to Wyatt shortly after Virgil was ambushed. Dake never faltered in his backing of the Earps. This is a portion of a Dake letter of December 3, 1881, to Acting Attorney General of the United States, S. F. Phillips; from the U. S. Marshals Collection, McLean, Virginia.

Tis true, the Sheriff of Cochise County (bordering on Sonora), in which Tombstone is situated, attempted to interfere with the Messrs. Earp and their assistants but the attempt has completely failed.—The Earps have rid Tombstone and neighborhood of the presence of this outlaw element.—They killed several Cowboys in Tombstone recently—and the Sheriff's faction had my deputies arrested—and after a protracted trial my deputies were vindicated and publicly complimented for their bravery in driving this outlaw element from this part of our territory. . . .I am proud to report that I have some of the best and bravest men in my employ in this hazardous business—men who are trusty and tried, and who strike fear into the hearts of these outlaws.

*　　*　　*

REVENGE BEGINS

There was an attempt to assassinate Virgil, and the following account, from the San Diego Union, of December 30, 1881, is a good summary of that event.

Tombstone, December 29. Last night about half-past eleven

106

Dake, as U.S. Marshal, was the leading law enforcement official in the Arizona Territory. He appointed Virgil Earp as Deputy U.S. Marshal. Arizona Historical Society

o'clock, as Deputy Marshal Earp was crossing Fifth street, between the Oriental saloon and the Eagle brewery, when in the middle of the street, he was fired upon with double-barreled shotguns, loaded with buckshot, by three men concealed in an unfinished building diagonally across on Allen street. Five shots were fired in rapid succession. Earp was wounded in the left arm just above the elbow, producing a longitudinal fracture of the bone. One shot struck him above the groin, coming out near the spine. The wounds are very dangerous and possibly mortal. The men ran through the rear of the building, and escaped in the darkness back of the Vizna hoisting works. Nineteen of the shots struck the side of the Eagle brewery, three going through the window, one shot passing about a foot over the heads of some men who were standing by a faro table. Long ago the cowboy gang threatened the lives of Mayor Clum, Judge Spicer, Marshal Williams, the Agent of Wells, Fargo & Co., the Earps, and Holliday, and this is an attempt to carry the threats into execution. Intense feeling exists in the minds of all the better class of citizens at this dastardly attempt at assassination.

* * *

Account, journal entry of December 28, 1881, George Whitwell Parsons.

Tonight about 11:30 Doc. G. [Goodfellow] had just left, and I thought couldn't have crossed the street, when four shots were fired in quick succession from very heavily charged guns, making a terrible noise and I thought were fired under my window, under which I quickly dropped, keeping the dobe wall between me and the outside till the fusilade was over.

I immediately thought Doc. had been shot and fired in return, remembering a late episode and knowing how pronounced he was on the Earp-Cowboy question. He had crossed though and passed Virgil Earp, who crossed to West side of 5th and was fired upon when in range of my window by men, 2 or 3, concealed in the timbers of the new 2 story adobe going up for the Huachuca Water Co. He did not fall, but recrossed to the Oriental and was taken from there to the Cosmopolitan, being hit with buckshot and badly wounded in left arm with flesh wound above left thigh.

Cries of "There they go," "Head them off" were heard, but the cowardly, apathetic guardians of the peace were not inclined to risk themselves, and the other brave men all more or less armed did nothing. Doc. had a close shave.

Van and I went to hospital for Doc. and got various things. Hotel well guarded, so much so that I had hard trouble to get to Earp's room. He [Virgil] was easy. Told him I was sorry for him. "It's Hell, isn't it!" said he. His wife was troubled. "Never mind, I've got one arm left to hug you with," he said.

* * *

Wyatt went into action at once, and the following two accounts explain how and when he received his commission as a Deputy U. S. Marshal.

Arizona Miner, December 30, 1881.

The following telegram was received at Marshal Dake's office this morning:

Tombstone, Dec. 29-Virgil Earp was shot by a concealed assassin last night. The wound is considered fatal. Telegraph me appointment with power to appoint deputies. Local authorities have done nothing. The lives of other citizens have been threatened.

WYATT EARP

Tombstone Daily Nugget, January 3, 1882.

Wyatt Earp has received the appointment of Deputy United States Marshal, vice, Virgil Earp. Marshal Dake telegraphed the appointment upon receipt of the news of Virgil's injuries.

*   *   *

In 1891, when Virgil applied for a military pension, he described the wounds received in the assassination attempt; below are some excerpts from his pension file in the National Archives.

My wounds were received in Arizona in the discharge of my duties as U. S. Deputy Marshal and Chief of Police all received about Dec 1881. My leg wound prevents my riding, I cramp in the wounded leg, I cannot walk to any extent. . .left arm is perfectly useless and helpless. The wound of my back, I think produces neuralgia of stomach. . .[Then, regarding his arm] There is shortening to fully extent of 4 inches. The forearm swinging in a loose and useless manner, with complete loss of power.

*   *   *

Wanting a freer hand, the Earps decided to discard their official position; the following is from the Phoenix Arizona Gazette, February 3, 1882.

Wyatt and Virgil Earp have tendered their resignation as deputies of United States Marshal Dake [in Prescott].

*   *   *

EXIT MORGAN

Morgan Earp was killed on March 18, 1882, in one of the bloody sequels to the shootout. The following terse words are from the diary of George Parsons, entry of March 19, 1882; Chafin (ed.), Parsons Diaries.

Another assassination last night about eleven o'clock. I heard the shots, two in number, but hearing so many after dark was not particularly startled, though I remarked to Redfern about it. Poor Morgan Earp was shot through by an unknown party—probably 2 or 3 in number—in Campbell & Hatch's, while playing pool with Hatch. The shots, 2, came through the ground window leading into the alley running to Fremont Street on East side of Otis & Co.'s store. George Berry received the spent ball in his thigh, sustaining a flesh wound. The second shot was fired apparently at Wyatt Earp.

Murderers got away of course, but it was and is quite evident who committed the deed. The man was [Frank] Stilwell in all probability. For two cowardly, sneaking attempts at murder, this and the shots at Virgil E. which I came nearly getting a dose, rank at the head. Morg lived about 40 minutes after being shot and died without a murmur. Bad times ahead now.

San Diego Union, March 23, 1882.

Morgan Earp, one of the principals in the shooting which

occurred on the 16th of last November, in which Frederick and Tom McLaury and Billy Clanton were killed, was shot at ten minutes of eleven tonight while playing billiards in Campbell and Hatch's saloon. Two shots were fired through a glass door: one, and the fatal shot, taking effect in the abdomen, passing through the body and shattering the spinal column. He died at twelve o'clock, midnight. The other shot was aimed at his brother Wyatt, United States Deputy Marshal, who was sitting on the opposite side of the room, the ball passing over his head and lodging in the wall. There is no clue to the assassins. The evidence shows that two or more were engaged in the assassination.

San Diego Union, March 24, 1882.

The Coroner's jury find that Morgan S. Earp came to his death at the hands of Frank Stilwell, who was killed the next day in Tucson, Pete Spencer, one of his friends, and two half-breed Indians. Pete Spencer's wife exposes the plot. A Sheriff's posse, consisting of twenty men, mostly Cowboys, left this morning for the Dragoon Mountains, where the Earps are supposed to be at present. The Sheriff made a weak attempt to arrest them at the Cosmopolitan Hotel before they left, but Wyatt Earp told him he didn't want to see him; that he had seen him once too often, and thereupon the Earp party mounted their horses and rode away. There is a very uneasy feeling among the Cowboy element, as the Earps are rendered desperate by the attempted assassination of Virgil Earp and the cold-blooded murder of Morgan Earp.

A detailed account of the entire Morgan episode appeared in the San Diego Union of March 31, 1882, by Clara Brown, the paper's Tombstone correspondent. Here are her words describing Morgan's final moments.

Frank Stilwell. Arizona Historical Society

Morgan fell to the floor, and was assisted to a lounge in the card room, where he died in less than an hour. The death scene is said to have been very affecting. The man was surrounded by his brothers and their wives, whose grief was intense. He whispered some words to Wyatt, which have not been given to the public, but spoke aloud only once, when his companions endeavored to raise him to his feet: "Don't, boys, don't," he said, "I can't stand it; I have played my last game of pool."

*   *   *

THE PENALTY FOR KILLING AN EARP

The attitude of the Earp gang, and their method of revenge against Stilwell, can be gathered by some of the comments in the following, from the San Diego Union of March 22, 1882. The Earps, and Holliday, had gone to Tucson, from where they were to put Morgan's body in charge of Virgil, for the trip home to Colton, California. At the train station in Tucson, someone spotted Stilwell, who may have been there on business, or may have been planning mischief against the Earps.

A few moments before the train started, Stilwell and Ike Clanton, brother of the Clanton who was killed at Tombstone by the Earps, went to the train to meet a man by the name of McDowell, who was to have come in as a witness before the Grand Jury. On their arrival at the depot they saw the Earp party walking on the platform. Stilwell advised Clanton to leave at once, saying they wanted to kill him. Clanton left a few minutes later. Stilwell was seen walking down the track in the direction where his body was found. Some of the armed men who were on the platform soon followed. One was described as a slender, light complex-ioned man, wearing a light hat. Just as the train was leaving, six shots were heard in the locality of the assassination, but attracted no particular attention, and nothing was known of the tragedy until this morning, when the body was discovered. Six shots went into his body, four rifle balls and two loads of buckshot. Both legs were shot through, and there was a charge of buckshot in his left thigh, and a charge through his breast, which must have been delivered close, as the coat was powder burnt, and there were six buckshot holes within a radius of three inches. Stilwell had a pistol on his person, which was not discharged.,

*   *   *

Years later, Sheriff Bob Paul was interviewed in Tomb-stone about the Stilwell incident; Tombstone Prospector, March 3, 1898.

The Earps did not follow Stilwell to Tucson. Ike Clanton and Frank Stilwell came to Tucson, and about two weeks later the Earps came on the train as an escort to Virgil Earp, who had been shot from rear of saloon on Allen street and was on his way to Colton, where his father and mother lived, for medical treatment. While the train was standing in Tucson, Frank Stilwell was seen standing on a gravel car peeking in the window of the car that Virgil Earp was in. Wyatt Earp and the balance of the escort started after him, overtook him and killed him. The train pulled out before the shooting was over.

*   *   *

The perpetrators of the ambush on Virgil Earp and the

Bob Paul's law and order career lasted more than half a century, in California and Arizona. He was Wells, Fargo employee and later Sheriff of Pima County while the Earps were in Tombstone. He later served as Deputy U.S. Marshal. Wells, Fargo History Room, San Francisco

assassination of Morgan Earp were never discovered. However, it seems that Will McLaury, brother of the two deceased McLaury brothers, knew about the shootings, and may have sponsored them. Will was an attorney from Fort Worth, who participated in the legal work at the examination of the Earps and Holliday. He was not pleased with the outcome. The following, from the New-York Historical Society Archives, is part of a letter from Will to his father, dated April 12, 1884.

My experience out there (Tombstone) has been very unfortunate as to my health and badly injured me as to money matters. And none of the results have been satisfactory. The only result is the death of Morgan and crippling of Virgil Earp and death of McMasters.

*   *   *

James Earp, a Tombstone saloon keeper not involved in the famous shootout, arrived in Los Angeles in late March of 1882. His long interview, which appeared in the Los Angeles Times of March 28, 1882, is interesting but similar to most other accounts of the shootout and vendetta. The opening paragraph, though, contains one of the few personal comments about James.

Yesterday James C. Earp and wife, of Tombstone, Arizona, registered at the Pico House, and in the afternoon Mr. Earp allowed a TIMES reporter a lengthy interview. He stated that he had just come from Colton, where he had been visiting his parents, and had buried his brother, Morgan, a week ago last Sunday. He had left Tombstone a few days previous in company with his and

Morgan's wife, bringing his brother's dead body to Colton for burial. Mrs. Morgan Earp is now with her parents-in-law at Colton. Mr. Earp is accompanied here by his wife, a very beautiful brunette. He himself is a blond, blue eyes, light hair, about five feet six inches high, rather stout of build, has a heavy mustache, and very neatly dressed.

*   *   *

Very little is known of Morgan's wife, Louisa. In the following paragraph, Morgan's sister, Adelia, comments on events at the time of Morgan's death; Adelia Earp Edwards Memoirs, Colton Public Library.

And we used to wonder about Morgan's wife too. When she heard he had been murdered, she went off to Arizona to bring his body back to Colton and only stayed with us a few weeks more after he was put to rest. She was a real, sad lady. I recall best that sad look in her eyes. But she was a fine person and a stunning looker, and she was waiting for Morg to come back from Tombstone when she heard. She just fell down on the floor and sobbed and sobbed. She lived in Tombstone a short time, but Morg sent her home to wait until they were ready to come home. I guess he was worried for her there. She was a clever young lady, had been to good schools. She just went away. We just don't know what became of her.

*   *   *

WYATT THE PURSUER

There does not deserve to be a dispute about whether or

**not the Earps carried the authority of the law—they did.
The dispute should be over whether or not they abused
their powers. A few days after Morgan's assassination,
Wyatt formed a posse. The following notice is from Martin,
Tombstone's Epitaph, but erroneously carries the date of
January 24, 1882; in reality, Mayor John Carr issued the
proclamation on March 24, 1882.**

To the citizens of the city of Tombstone: I am informed by his
Honor, William H. Stilwell, Judge of the District Court of the first
Judicial District, Cochise County, that Wyatt S. Earp, who left the
city yesterday with a posse, was intrusted with warrants for the
arrest of divers persons charged with criminal offenses. I request
the public within this city to abstain from any interference with
the execution of said warrants.

*　　*　　*

**One wonders about the cause of the fracas in the San
Bernardino bank, as reported in this account in the Los
Angeles Herald of December 1, 1881. Chances are, someone
said something nasty about one of the Earp boys, in
Tombstone, and Nick Earp replied in kind.**

An exciting scene took place Monday afternoon in front of the
Exchange Bank. Old man Earp, who was under the influence of
liquor, was in the bank and became very abusive to Mr. Byron
Waters, who turned him out of the building. When on the
sidewalk he continued his abuse, and for some time Mr. Waters
took no notice of him. He continued it for some time, using the
vilest language and applying the vilest epithets, until Mr. Waters,
who was unable to stand his abuse any long, jumped over the

119

counter and knocked him down. Then the Marshal appeared upon the scene, picked the old fellow up and took him off.

*   *   *

WYATT: THE PURSUER PURSUED

Sheriff Robert Paul of Pima County became involved in the Earp-cowboy feud because Stilwell was killed in Tucson, seat of Pima County. Paul was a close friend of Wyatt Earp and was less than luke-warm about pursuing him. The following accounts indicate Paul's reluctant role.

Los Angeles Times, March 28, 1882.

Sheriff Paul has returned from Tombstone. He says that he did not go in pursuit of the Earps, because the posse selected by Sheriff Behan, of Tombstone, were mostly hostile to the Earps and that a meeting meant bloodshed without any probability of arrest. Sheriff Paul says the Earps will come to Tucson and surrender to the authorities.

Los Angeles Times, May 17, 1882.

EARP PARTY ARRESTED AND HELD AT DENVER Sheriff Paul today received a dispatch from the Sheriff at Denver, Col., stating that he had arrested and held in custody the Earp party, who are indicted in the county (Pima) for the murder of Frank Stilwell. There are five men in the party. Tipton, one of the party, met a violent death in New Mexico two weeks ago, while attempting a robbery. Governor Tritle placed a requisition in the hands of Sheriff Paul, who leaves for Denver for the prisoners to-morrow

morning. Perfect quiet has reigned in Cochise county since the
Earp party left.

*　*　*

VIRGIL RECOVERS

Los Angeles Times, May 28, 1882.

Virgil W. Earp, of Arizona fame, is now in San Francisco. He
came here for surgical treatment. In his last fight he received a
wound in the left arm by a bullet, which caused the loss of about
six inches of bone, that will probably cripple him for life. He will
have an operation performed on the limb. In conversation Earp
admitted that his party killed Stilwell.

*　*　*

**The San Francisco Daily Examiner of May 27, 1882,
carried a long, detailed article-interview with focus on
Virgil and his Tombstone career. The cowboy feud, the
relations with Sheriff Behan, the shootout—all are covered,
and resemble most other reliable sources. Following are a
few excerpts that provide descriptions of Virgil's appearance and personality.**

Virgil Earp is not a ruffian in appearance. He was found in a
sleeping car, smoking a cigar. His face, voice and manner were
prepossessing. He is close to six feet in height, of medium build,
chestnut hair, sandy mustache, light eyebrows, quiet, blue eyes
and frank expression. He wore a wide-brimmed, slate-colored
slouch hat, pants of a brown and white stripe, and a blue diagonal

121

coat and vest, both the latter with bullet holes in them, bearing testimony of a recent fight when he was shot in the back, the bullet coming out at the front of his vest. His left arm was carried in a sling, also a memento of his last fight, when he received a bullet in his arm, since causing the loss of about six inches of bone and which cripples him for life.

"We went into Tombstone to do our duty as officers. To do that we were put in conflict with a band of desperadoes, and it resolved itself into a question of which side could first drive the other out of the country, or kill them in it. To-day my brother Morg is dead, and I am a cripple for life. My other brothers are fugitives, but they will give themselves up. It was our boys who killed Stilwell."

"The stories, at one time widely circulated, that we were in with the cowboys and quarreled over the division of the spoils, was ridiculous. It was at least disbelieved by Wells, Fargo & Co., who I represented, and while I was City Marshal they gave me this." The speaker here displayed on the inside of his coat a large gold badge, a five-pointed star set inside of a circular band, inscribed on one side, "City Marshal, Tombstone, A. T.," and on the other, "V. W. Earp, with Compliments of Wells, Fargo & Co." Mr. Earp was in such pain that for the time his story was cut short.

*　　*　　*

OFFICIAL BLESSINGS

The acting governor of Arizona Territory, John Gosper, and the U. S. Marshal, Crawley P. Dake, vigorously backed the Earp faction, claiming that the Cochise County Sheriff, Johnny Behan, was in cahoots with the cowboys. Lending credibility to that point of view is that the new governor,

122

John Gosper, a former roommate of Doc Holliday in Prescott, was Acting Governor and was friendly to the Clum-Earp faction. General John Fremont was governor of Arizona Territory during the Tombstone troubles, but spent most of his time out of the territory. Arizona Quarterly Illustrated, July, 1880

Frederick A. Tritle, took the same position. The following is from an interview with Tritle, from the Tucson Star, April 21, 1882, long after the Earps had anything to do with Territory affairs.

The governor expressed his determination to put down lawlessness in the Territory if the people would give him any thing like a fair support in the undertaking. He said with truth that the state of affairs that has existed in Cochise county for some time past was a disgrace to civilization and that the facts of the matter should be promptly laid before Congress and that body requested to appropriate sufficient funds to put down cattle stealing and smuggling. . . .When he asked for power to suspend county officers he did it in no arbitrary spirit, but simply as an axe he could hold over the necks of officials in case of malfeasance in office. He said that if it was generally known that he was possessed of that power county officers would be more careful in attending to their duty; but by the present loose arrangements county officials are practically their own bosses, therefore do about as they please.

CHAPTER 3
AFTERMATH, FLIGHT, FAME

San Diego Union, May 28, 1882, copied from Colton Semi-Tropic.

From Mr. V. W. Earp, who is now a resident of Colton, and who, within the past three days, has received letters from his brothers, we learn that both Wyatt and Warren Earp are alive and well, and are ready, when there is a reasonable show of justice being done them, to come before the courts, and stand trial for all charges that may be brought against them. N. P. Earp and his wife, the father and mother of the Earp boys, are residents of Colton, as are also two of the boys, James and Virgil, and a quieter, more law abiding family we do not often meet, and from them we learn all that they seek for themselves and brothers is simple justice.

* * *

Nick Earp was active in Colton, California, where in addition to running a saloon he also served as justice of the peace.
Colton Semi-Tropic, November 27, 1880

The following two brief news items need no comment.

Phoenix Arizona Gazette, July 27, 1882.

Virgil Earp is in business in San Francisco.

Phoenix Arizona Gazette, August 10, 1882.

126

Virgil Earp, of Tombstone notoriety, was arrested last Tuesday in San Francisco, on a charge of dealing faro. Over $1,000 and a "lay out" was captured with him.

*   *   *

In 1883, Dodge City saloon man Luke Short got into a legal tangle with city officials, who tried to run him out of town. Short put out the word, and "friends" from throughout the West came to his aid. The "Dodge City War" never happened, but Short's friends did appear, and the following comments during the year suggest that the new arrivals helped quiet the town.

Kansas City Journal, May 15, 1883.

[Masterson's] presence in Kansas City means just one thing, and that is he is going to visit Dodge City. Masterson precedes by twenty-four hours a few other pleasant gentlemen who are on their way to the tea party at Dodge. One of them is Wyatt Earp. . .famous in the cheerful business of depopulating the country. He has killed within our personal knowledge six men, and is popularly accredited with relegating to the dust no less than ten of his fellow men.

Ford County Globe, June 12, 1883.

Wyatt Earp, a former marshal of Dodge City, arrived in the city from the west, last Thursday. Wyatt is looking well and glad to get back to his old haunts, where he is well and favorably known.

Ford County Globe, November 13, 1883.

The famous "Dodge City Peace Commission" was just a collection of buddies of Luke Short, called back from various Western parts to Dodge City in 1883, where Luke needed some backing. Wyatt is seated, second from left. Colton Public Library

B. Masterson, formerly sheriff and ex-city marshal, and Wyat Earp, ex-city marshal of this city quietly and unostentatiously dropped in onto our inhabitants early last Tuesday morning, and their presence about the polls on that day had a moral effect on our would-be moral element, that was truly surprising. It is needless to say every thing passed off quietly at the city precinct on election day.

* * *

The following, from the San Diego Union of August 16, 1884, is interesting for revealing Nick Earp's political activity, and also shows his running mate—Bryon Waters, party to the drunken brawl with Nick on the sidewalks of San Bernardino a few years earlier.

N. P. Earp, father of the Earp boys who made things so lively in Tombstone some two or three years ago, was nominated for County Recorder by the Democratic County Convention which met in San Bernardino last Tuesday. The same convention nominated Byron Waters for Superior Judge and William A. Harris for the Assembly.

* * *

IDAHO CALLING

Wyatt, James, and Warren hit for the Idaho gold fields in early 1884, where Wyatt and James, in addition to owning mining claims, also operated a saloon, the "White Elephant." The following land transaction was printed in Idaho Yesterdays, Fall, 1967.

129

Know all men by these presents—That We, Sanford and Owens of Eagle City, Shoshone County, Idaho Territory, parties of the 1st part, for and in consideration of the sum of One Hundred and Thirty Two Dollars to them in hand paid by Wyatt S. Earp, James C. Earp, J. E. Emory, and H. Holman of Eagle City, parties of the 2d part—the receipt whereof is hereby acknowledged, have this day sold and delivered and by these presents do humbly sell and declare unto said parties of the 2d part the following property situate in Eagle City—to wit: One tent with poles door and floor situated at Cor North of S. H Hayes store and immediately adjoining same. The stove pipe, tables, chares, benches, bar and bar fixtures therein contained together with all stock in said building contained with all lamps Schandelires and their fixtures. To have and to hold the same forever . . . .

Dated April 26th 1884 Eagle City, Idaho Sanford and Owens

*   *   *

In the Idaho mining fields, the Earps lined up with Charles Sweeney; together they entered tough legal confrontations with A. J. Pritchard. The following is from Fahey, The Ballyhoo Bonanza, giving an historian's assessment of the Earps in Idaho.

Sweeney and the Earps emerged as local heroes because their action was regarded as a test of legitimacy of a number of claims staked on behalf of absentees. . . .Sweeney, with the Earp brothers, apparently undertook to resolve Pritchard's claim on behalf of the whole camp.

*   *   *

LOOSE ENDS OF THE 1880s

Arizona Journal-Miner, June 23, 1886.

Virgil Earp, a former resident of Prescott, and who became famous in connection with the cowboy troubles in Southern Arizona, is running a detective bureau in Colton, California.

*   *   *

San Bernardino Daily Times, January 22, 1887.

Mrs. James Earp, who has been ailing for some time, died at her residence this morning.

*   *   *

Just as in Lamar, Missouri, where Nick as Justice and Wyatt as Constable had a good thing going, the method was repeated in Colton, where Nick was Justice of the Peace, and Virgil got hired as a constable; from San Bernardino Weekly Times, February 12, 1887.

Constable Earp brought up from Colton this morning eight tramps who had been sentenced to ten days each by Justice Earp of Colton. They were captured asleep in a box car and the tax payers have got to put up some ten to fifteen dollars each for them in Justice fees, constable fees, board and attention.

*   *   *

131

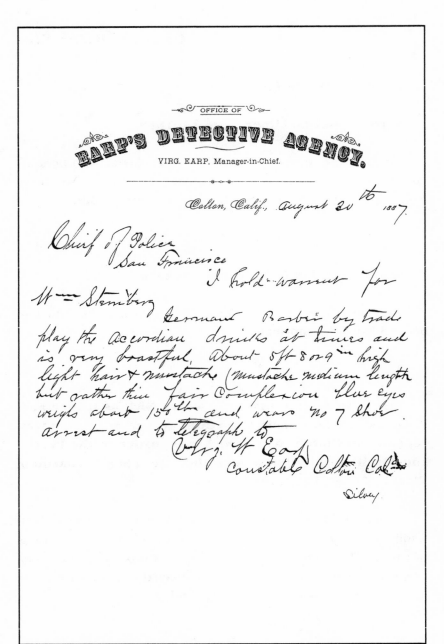

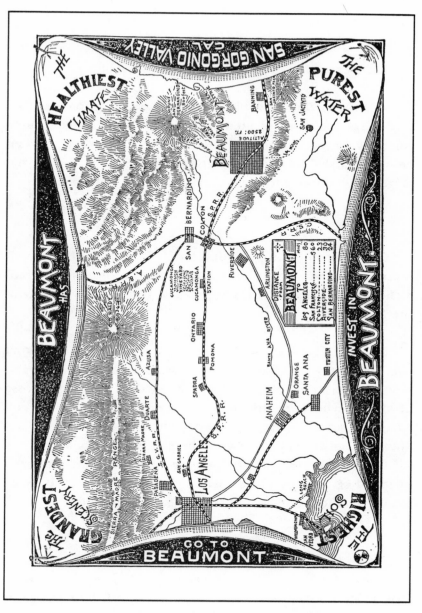

Justice Nick Earp and Chief of Police Virgil Earp were kept busy in Colton, crossroads of two major railroad lines. Natural History Museum, Los Angeles

133

San Bernardino Daily Times, July 14, 1887.

V. W. Earp, the newly elected City Marshal [Colton], sports a gold badge that was presented to him by the Wells, Fargo express company for services done at Tombstone, A. T., years ago, when he was Marshal of that city. It is a beauty and cost in the neighborhood of eighty dollars.

*   *   *

Ike Clanton, who provided much of the anti-Earp testimony at the shootout inquest, like most of his family, had a checkered career. This clipping, of June 9, 1887, is from the Sharlot Hall Museum.

IKE CLANTON DEAD J. H. O'Neil, a deputy sheriff from Graham county arrived in the city yesterday from Maricopa and reported the killing of Ike Clanton, a few days since, by a posse of officers who were attempting to secure his arrest, on several charges of grand larceny. The particulars of the killing were not obtained, but as to the occurence there seems to be no doubt. Ike Clanton will be remembered as one of several brothers who operated extensively in Cochise county about five or six years since and who was regarded as a dangerous character.

*   *   *

Justice Spicer, who delivered the Earp-Holliday decision after the famous Tombstone shootout, had at best a mixed career. Following are before and after views of a key player in the Tombstone drama.

Tombstone Nugget, June 24, 1880.

Wells Spicer, Esq., has been appointed by Chief Justice French, U. S. Court Commissioner, for the first district of the territory of Arizona. His court will have jurisdiction for all criminal cases against the United States, and for the violation of Internal Revenue and Custom laws. The appointment is a proper one.

Arizona Daily Star, April 13, 1887.

DISAPPEARED. About three months ago Judge Spicer left the Quijota for Covered Wells. While there he visited Bill Hayne's cabin and made two attempts to commit suicide but was prevented by Haynes. He told Haynes there were other ways to kill himself, and leaving the cabin struck out for the mountains. Haynes offered him grub stake to take with him, but he refused to take any. Since that time nothing has been heard of him in any of the surrounding camps and the supposition is that he has perished from exposure. Parties have written from Quijota to Casa Grande in regard to him, but he has not put in an appearance there. In fact nothing has been heard from him nor has anyone seen him since he left Hayne's cabin.

*   *   *

Virgil's crippled condition did not seem to affect his job performance as Colton marshal; from the memoirs of Adelia Earp Edwards, Colton Public Library.

There was some trouble in Colton when Virgil was marshal. That was in 1887, I think. But it was mainly young drunks, no real trouble.

135

One time, one of these swaggering types made some remark about Virge's crippled arm. In about a tick of the clock, he was off his feet, right up off the street and onto the sidewalk, and pretty hard up against the wall, spread-eagled. Virgil did all this in one move, with one arm. He sure was a strong feller! He just frisked this young drunk a bit rough and pushed him away, and said "Now you just run along home, boy."

*   *   *

In an unusual move, the new Colton City Marshal left for Arizona; from Tombstone Epitaph, August 20, 1887.

Virgil Earp, city marshal of Colton, Cal., was in Fairbank (near Tombstone) last Sunday, looking for train robbers.

*   *   *

Fred Dodge explains the above situation; Fred was after two train robbers and telegraphed to Tombstone for help. He recounted the following in Under Cover for Wells, Fargo.

About the first one that I heard from was Virgil Earp, who was in Tombstone—Charley Smith and I both wanted to see the Old Boy badly. He come down on the Stage and we met him at Benson. Virgil Earp had been in California Ever since they tried to assassinate him when he was City Marshal in Tombstone.

That Evening, close to dark, we had got word of two men Horseback on the Rincon Mountains, and we were going to leave for there before daylight in the Morning. Virg wanted to go with us, so we got him a good horse and outfit at Benson and we all left before day.

Virg had shown us his Arm and told us all about how it had got along--the Surgeons had taken out the whole Elbow and there was nothing there but flesh. Manuel had been out among the Mexicans, Scouting for information, and had only met Virg a few minutes that night. In the morning, as we were nearing the Rincons, we had an open Mesa to cross and we were Crossing it at a good Stiff gallop, so that we would be past it before it got light enough to be seen from a distance Virg had let his arm dangle and he noticed Manuel observing him closely, So he let his arm flog around for Virg knew how Supersticious this Class of Indian and Mexican was, and in a few Minutes, Manuel Come rushing up to me with, "My God, Boss, what is that matter with that Man?" I knew Manual and his suppersticions, and as we were where we Could ease up or Stop and not be seen, I had to Stop the whole outfit and get Virg to get off of his horse and Show Manuel his arm, and then we told him all about it. He had heard of it and was very much interested. He felt of the arm, lifted it up, and was very much impressed--and he and Virg become great friends. He looked out for Virg on all occasions and took care of Virg's horse for him on the whole trip.

(They never located the train robbers.)

*　　*　　*

Virgil and Allie, although not apparently officially married, had one of the longest unions of any of the Earps. The following land record, part of the Earp Papers in the Colton Public Library, is testimony to the closeness of the relationship.

137

I, Virgil W. Earp, of the City of Colton, County of San Bernardino, and State of California, for and in consideration of the love and affection which I bear towards my wife and as an expression of my heartfelt gratitude to her for her constant, patient and heroic attendance at my bedside while I lay dangerously wounded at Tombstone, Arizona, do grant unto my wife, Mrs. Alvira Earp, as her separate estate, all that real property situated in the City of Colton, County of San Bernardino, State of California, described as follows, to wit: Lots numbered five (5) and six (6) in Block number one hundred and thirteen (113) in and of said City of Colton, being the same lots conveyed to me by J. F. Walin, by deed bearing date April 30, 1888, and now of record at page 112 in Vol. 14 of deeds, records of said San Bernardino County.

Witness my hand this 7th day of July, 1888.

Virgil W. Earp

*   *   *

San Bernardino Weekly Times, July 28, 1888.

Nelgan and Weber are being tried by Judge Earp of Colton on a charge of residing in a house of ill fame.

*   *   *

In 1888, H. H. Bancroft, in compiling data for his massive history publication project, sent his agent G. W. Caldwell to interview Wyatt Earp, then living in San Diego. The interview, now in the Bancroft Library, Berkeley, follows, and is permeated with Wyatt's high self-esteem.

138

Alvira "Allie" Earp, as petite as Virgil was grand, was inseparable from him as they wandered the West in search of whatever the Earps hoped to find. Natural History Museum, Los Angeles

Wyatt portrait as in San Diego, late 1880s. San Diego Public Library

WYATT S. EARP. Born in Monmouth Ills. March 19th 1848. Came to California with his parents 1864. Home of parents, Colton, Cal. Was U. S. Dep. Marshal in Arizona. Special officer for Fargo & Wells. Has Killed over a dozen stage robbers, murderers, and cattle thieves. To him more than any other man is due the credit for driving out the banditti of that territory. He is tall, slim, florid complexion, blue eyes, large nose, & quick as a cat. Socially he could be taken for a Minister. He has a heart as big as an ox and feelings as tender as a child. Is worth $30,000, owns property in San Diego, Tombstone, & has about $6000 or $7000 cash.

Bancroft's man interviewed Virgil in Colton in 1888, and the result is a three-page amalgam of heroic deeds, exaggeration, and fantasy. Extracts follow; from Bancroft Library.

In 1874 Mr. Earp went to Wichita Kansas, which was then looked upon as being one of the harshest towns in the west and known as the Cattle drive. At that time there were a great many desperadoes in the town. Mr. Earp being a man of undoubted Courage was frequently called upon to protect the interests of his neighbors as well of his own against their depredations. . . In 1879 Mr. Earp went to Tombstone Arz for the same purpose of protecting property against the desperations of the outlaws, at which time Mr. Earp was elected deputy U. S. Marshall and in Company with his two brothers Morgan and Wyat Earp did very creditable Services in bringing the greater portion of this band of outlaws to justice and Compelling the remainder of the band through the Vigilance of the Earp brothers to seek new fields for their nefarious operations. . . .Mr. Earp is now 43 years of age and is respected and admired in the Community in which he lives as a man of sterling worth, strong sense of justice and fearless in the

141

discharge of his duty. Mr. Earp has been wounded nine times in his defense of life and property, in one of his engagements his brother Morgan Earp was killed. Mr. Earp's father was a scout under Daniel Boone.

* * *

A few dollars came Wyatt's way for officiating at various sporting events. The following, from the Los Angeles Tribune of June 2, 1888, concerns a boxing match across the border in Tijuana, Mexico, onlookers including children, "burly sailors," and a "half-drunken mob," to see two fellows named O'Neil and Nugent slam away at each other.

There was an upheaval in the midst of the intertwined fighters, and the two plucky officers struggled to their feet, with their backs to a wall, and leveled their cocked revolvers at the crowd. It was not a very pleasant assemblage to be in at its best, and at this point I felt a little uncomfortable. One never can judge what a course a bullet will take when fired into a crowd; particularly is that a difficult problem when you are one of the crowd. However, the mob was a cowardly one, and the prospect of being killed did not seem attractive. The referee, who was Wyatt Earp, made his appearance, and in a few words told the assemblage that they would not be disappointed; that the ring would be pitched on Mexican soil, and that the fight would surely come off. Earp has a cemetery which he has stocked with over 30 men, and no one seemed desirous of questioning his word.

* * *

142

J. M. ROBINSON, ATTORNEY. Practices in all Federal and State Courts, Special attention given to defective titles of all kinds before the departments at Washington, D. C.

E

Eadon E. H., Post Office News Stand, P. O., res 1151 First
Eadon William H., Coroner, res 1151 First
Ealy Mrs. K., clerk, Commercial Hotel, res same
Earle Frank S., res 663 Eleventh
Earp Wyatt, capitalist, res Schmitt Block
East Public School, S. D. LAND AND TOWN CO.'S addn
　Mary G. Phelps, teacher, third division; M. F. Hann, teacher, fourth division; Eliza Lundergreen, teacher, fifth division and principal.
Eaton A. C., contractor, res 1248 Fifth
Eaton Mrs. Fanny R., res 1803 B
Eaton Miss Flora, milliner, with Mrs. S. A. Williamson, res 1136 Fourth

• *Wyatt had come a long way by the time he settled in San Diego in the late 1880s, with this new "occupation."* Directory of San Diego, 1889-1890

Nick Earp was active in Democratic politics; from the San Bernardino Daily Times, August 30, 1888.

DEMOCRATIC RALLY. Colton had a rousing meeting last night at the Trans-continental hotel. San Bernardino sent a goodly delegation accompanied by the Seventh Regiment band; they were met by the Colton club upon their arrival in that town, and escorted to the place of meeting. Judge Earp introduced, with a few remarks, the speaker, Reel B. Terry, who spoke for an hour upon the political issues of the day.

*　　*　　*

Some of the doings of Justice of the Peace Nicholas Earp were reported in the Phoenix Herald, November 12, 1888.

A warrant of arrest was issued this morning for the arrest of a man by the name of Sturenberg, at Colton, for assault with a deadly weapon on a Chinaman in the Colton Hotel, on Saturday evening. Sturenberg went immediately to Judge Earp, after the fracas, and offered to pay a fine of $5, but it was not accepted, and the prospects are that the defendant will have to answer for a serious affair, as the Chinaman's skull was nearly broken with a hatchet.

*　　*　　*

WYATT'S NON-WIFE

Wyatt's women have figured in several books and magazine articles. Other than his marriage in 1870 to Rilla Sutherland in Lamar, there is no record of any further marriage. In Dodge City, he joined with Mattie (Cely Ann) Blalock (or Blylock), and she accompanied him to Tombstone, and was with him until he fell for Josephine Marcus. After the shootout Mattie accompanied other Earps from Tombstone to Colton. The following, gathered by Glenn G. Boyer for Suppressed Murder, focuses on Mattie.

(1860 Census, Monroe Township, Johnson County, Iowa)
Blylock, Henry   40   M   Ohio

144

Blylock, Elizabeth	31	F	Ind.
Blylock, Martha	17	F	Ind.
Blylock, Cele A.	10	F	Iowa
Blylock, Sarah	7	F	Iowa
Blylock, Wm. H.	5	M	Iowa

(Portion of land mortgage, Cochise County, Arizona)
Wyatt Earp et al To James G. Howard, February 13, '82
This indenture made the 13th day of February in the year of Our Lord one thousand eight hundred and eighty-two between Wyatt S. Earp and Mattie Earp, his wife and James G. Howard. . . .B. L. Peel, a Notary Public in and for the said County of Cochise personally appeared Mattie Earp (the wife of Wyatt S. Earp) whose name is subscribed to the foregoing instrument as a party personally known to me to be the person whose name is subscribed in and who executed the foregoing instrument as a party thereto;

/S/ B. L. Peel Notary Public

Filed and recorded at request of J. G. Howard
Feb. 14 A. D. 1882 at 10 A.M.

Mattie drifted into prostitution. This is how she met her end; from Pinal County, Arizona, Coroner's Inquest, "In the matter of the inquisition held upon the body of Mattie Earp deceased."

Q What is your name, age, occupation and residence:
A My name is Frank Beeler. I am 65 years of age. I am a laborer and live in Pinal, Arizona.
Q State to this jury all that you know about the cause of the death of the deceased.

145

A The woman felt sick and I knew pretty well what the sickness was as I had waited on her once before when she was the same way. I went to her room here in Pinal day before yesterday and looked in the door. I asked her if she wanted anything. She was lying in bed and a man was lying there on the bed beside her. During the day I did not go in there again but yesterday I went there about 8 or 9 o'clock in the morning. She was lying on the bed and I asked her if she wanted anything and she said come in here and sit down I want to talk to you. I went in and sat down and she said she didn't feel well and pointed around beside to the stand to a beer bottle that stood there. I took the bottle out. It contained whiskey about one fourth full. And she and I drank it up. She said then that she wanted to get more whiskey and some opium or laudanum as she wanted to try and get some sleep. while she was lying there I said where are your bracelets and she said i guess they are around here somewhere. I couldn't find them but found her breastpin and put it up on the wall. She said I would like to have you go to Luedke's and get me some laudanum as I cannot sleep. She then said go to Werners' and get more whiskey. I went there and got fifty cents worth of whiskey and took it to her. Then she wanted me to go and get the laudanum. I went to Luedke and he gave me a small bottle of laudanum and I took it to her. . . .I sat there about an hour and then went in the other room as I was feeling the liquor. I laid down and about that time Flannery came to the door and I then went out and I was gone about two hours when I went back to her house and as I wanted a drink I looked around for the whiskey but couldn't find any and the whole bottle of laudanum was gone. I felt her pulse and her heart and they seemed to be beating allright and she seemed to be asleep. I sat down then for an hour or two and then went out as I thought she was asleep. I was away about two hours and then went back and

146

saw a number of persons there. The Dr. was one of them and seemed to be trying to restore her.

. . . .Subscribed and sworn to before me this 4th day of July A.D. 1888. W. H. Burson, Acting Coroner, Pinal County, Arizona

*   *   *

Florence Arizona Enterprise, July 7, 1888.

Mattie Earp, a frail denizen of Pinal, culminated a big spree by taking a big dose of laudanum, on Tuesday, and died from its effects. She was buried on the 4th.

*   *   *

Extract of a letter, Mabel Earp Cason to Mrs. Wm. Irvine, April 16, 1959, copy in Colton Public Library.

I was rather surprised at the transcript of the inquiry into Mattie Earp's death. Poor thing, she seems to have let herself go completely. Allie Earp, Virgil's wife, thought a great deal of her and so I suppose before he deserted her she was a respectable woman. I still wonder if they were ever married. They were together for at least 10 or 12 years.

*   *   *

U. S. Marshal Crawley Dake was a strong partisan of Virgil Earp, arranging to have him created Deputy U. S. Marshal. After the Tombstone shootout, and the attempt to

assassinate Virgil, Dake appointed Wyatt Earp a Deputy U. S. Marshal. Portions of the following letter, from Jas. A. Zabriskie, U. S. Attorney, Tucson, to Benjamin Harris, Attorney General of the United States, January 22, 1885, not only clarify Wyatt's official status, but show the fix Dake was in; Earp Papers, Spec. Collections, University of Arizona.

The defendant Dake claims, and I believe with a great deal of truth, that the money for which his accounts are short was disbursed by Deputy Marshal Earp during the great excitement which prevailed in southern Arizona, over the "cow-boy" raids, and depredations at the incipiency of Governor Tritle's administration. The country was almost in a state of revolution, and a reign of terror existed at the time. Deputy Marshal Earp was very active in his efforts to suppress this "quasi" insurrection and prevent the violation of United States laws, and the contest became so bitter and violent that, as you remember, President Arthur, at the request of Govenor Tritle, placed the Territory under Martial law.

Deputy Marshal Earp and his band killed quite a number of these cow-boys, and a regular vendetta war ensued between the Marshal and his posse, and the combined force of the cow-boy element throughout the southern portion of the Territory. Mr. Earp finally resigned and left the Territory, and subsequently these discordant elements were suppressed, after great exertion, chiefly by the United States Authorities. Marshal Dake came down from Prescott to the scene of the disorders in this part of the country, near the close of the struggle, and gave matters his personal attention; Earp and his party being then in the mountains, pursuing and pursued. Dake did not see Earp again, as he did not return to Tombstone, but went into New Mexico and subsequently to Colorado, where he disappeared for the time being.

Now, Marshal Dake, claims that he has never been able to settle with the Government, because he has been unable to see Deputy Earp since, and obtain from him vouchers for all of the expenses, as Earp was really driven out of the country by the enemies of the Government, and sent his resignation to Marshal Dake, by mail.

*   *   *

Dake's financial mess came near the end of his life; the following is from a newspaper clipping, Sharlot Hall Museum.

DAKE.—In Prescott, April 9, 1890. C. P. Dake, a native of Canada, age 52. Deceased was one of the first men in Michigan who raised a company for the late war. It was incorporated in the Michigan Fifth Cavalry and the gallant regiment had no braver soldier than Captain, afterwards Major C. P. Dake. It was while fighting in its ranks that he received a wound which for years caused him great pain and which finally caused his death. He was U. S. Marshal of Arizona at a time when parts of the south were afflicted with desperadoes, whose career he greatly aided in bringing to an end.

Coming to Arizona, he was appointed United States marshal for the territory, at a time, too, when it required tact and nerve to fill the position, but the duties of which were discharged by him in a manner to reflect credit. Since retiring from this office, he has been engaged in business pursuits until over a year ago, when he was compelled to retire on account of sickness and has ever since been confined to the house.

*   *   *

149

THOSE SPORTING MEN, THE EARPS

Wyatt and Virgil officiated at many boxing, wrestling, and racing events. The following, from the San Bernardino Daily Courier of December 28, 1889, shows Virgil's local reputation.

Cotton and Sullivan are to fight again. The day is named, the place fixed, the articles signed. . . .They will fight in the Opera house on the night of January 18th, and as to Cotton's stipulation, that Virgil Earp shall be referee, Sullivan says it suits him exactly, as two of the Earp boys have refereed for him in two of his hardest fights.

* * *

However, Virgil, who had organized, sponsored, and refereed the first fight, realized in the second fight that the match was being "thrown," and pretty much killed boxing in San Bernardino for some time; from San Bernardino Weekly Courier, January 25, 1890.

Mr. Earp, who saw how things were going, refused to be a party to such a foul fooling of the audience, and would not notice a foul, upon which Cotton threw off his gloves. No man in San Bernardino would pay five cents to see either Sullivan or Cotton, or both, fight again.

* * *

San Diego Daily Sun, October 2, 1890, mentions one of the preoccupations of the Earp brothers. This referred to

150

horse races at the Escondido Fair, a few miles north of San Diego.

By time the races were called at 2 o'clock yesterday the track had been worked into good condition though it was a little soft and therefore a little slow. Wyatt Earp, James A. Jasper and A. D. Graham were selected as judges.

*   *   *

In the late 1880s, while living in San Diego, Wyatt decided to cash in on the gold excitement in the Harquahala Mountains, in modern La Paz County, Arizona. The following accounts show how he tried, but his success was minimal.

San Diego Union, January 24, 1889.

William Bryson and Wyatt Earp have returned from the Harqua Hala mines, and give a glowing account of that district and also the information that they have established a townsite there.

Clipping on Harqua Hala, dated February 12, 1889, probably from Tombstone Prospector, and included in Winter, Forgotten Mines and Treasures, p. 50.

A well was sunk close to the big ledge and an abundance of water struck at the depth of thirty feet. There are two mixed stores there and on the way out Peterman met Wyatt Earp going in with an immense load of bar fixtures and liquors, accompanied by two women. Earp thinks it is going to be the biggest boom ever seen on the Pacific coast and goes prepared to build a substantial building. He will locate near the mine, where the water was struck, and endeavor to draw others to that spot and start a town there.

Arizona Sentinel, May 11, 1889.

The two claims which have made the great excitement are known as the Gold Hill and the Golden Eagle. They are a mile apart. The Gold Hill being that far west of the Eagle. . . .There is neither grass or water at the mines. The water used at the camp costs $1 per barrel, and is hauled out from Harrisburg. Everything in the vicinity that looks like quartz is located, and some very promising prospects have been found and dug upon a little. There are at the Bonanza camp and Harrisburg perhaps 100 men. . . .

Wyatt Earp has a shaft down 110 feet when I left, sinking for water, a mile below the Gold Hill.

San Diego Union, July 30, 1889.

Wyatt S. Earp and William B. Bryson returned Sunday evening from Harqua Hala, A.T., driving the entire distance overland across the Colorado desert. Their description of the back country of San Diego is very flattering, saying that very few have any idea of its magnitude or fertility, commencing some 150 miles back. The mining camp of Harqua Hala, over which there was considerable excitement here several months since, is now at a standstill owing to the want of capital for its development. They report the quartz mines as good ones, and will at some future day make a great output. Messrs. Earp and Bryson have several good claims there, and will probably return to that camp next fall.

*   *   *

152

Nicholas Earp, living in Colton, was a long-time Justice of the Peace, business man, and participant in local politics and veterans affairs. The following, about a gathering of Civil War soldiers, appeared in the San Bernardino Daily Courier of October 27, 1889, is typical of the frequent coverage he received in the local press.

The exercises were opened by an old-time minuet, led by four tender urchins just a little in advance of the pinafore age, who are noted for the easy grace with which they carry themselves through the giddy mazes of the dance. These frisky boys are Judge N. P. Earp, Uncle Billy Head, Capt. C. A. Collins and Major G. W. Suttenfield.

*　　*　　*

Colton Chronicle, January 19, 1895.

The Pioneers held another of those jolly meetings for which they have become famous and elected the following named officers for the year. President, George Lord; Vice Presidents, N. P. Earp, W. F. Holcomb and B. B. Harris; Corresponding Secretary, Marcus Katz; Secretary, John Brown, Jr.; Treasurer, B. B. Harris; Marshal, William Stephen.

*　　*　　*

The following note, from the San Luis Obispo Tribune of September 11, 1891, is interesting for what it does not say. Virgil and his wife were not "beaching it," they were following the California autumn horse racing circuit.

153

Virgie Earp of San Bernardino, formerly deputy United States marshal and chief of police at Tombstone, Arizona, and the gamest man of his day, is at Santa Maria, on his way to this city. He and Mrs. Earp will spend a month or two at the beach.

* * *

His horse most likely came in last. The following letter, from Virgil's pension claim, indicates a contemplated change of residence that never happened.

OFFICE OF THE COSMOPOLITAN HOTEL, Jos. Frederick, Proprietor, Monterey Street, San Luis Obispo, Cal., Oct. 4th, 1891

Green B. Brown Commissioner

Washington D.C.

Dear Sir

You will take notice from the above heading that I have changed my residence from San Bernardino Calif. to San Luis Obispo California.

Yours Respectfully

Virgil W Earp

Late of Co C 83 Ill Inf

Claim No 954-186

Under Act June 27, 1890

* * *

By the early 1890s, the comings-and-goings of the Earps were subject to many newspaper and magazine notices. This typical brief blurb appeared in the Carson City Morning Appeal, January 9, 1892.

154

The Santa Rosa Island, only twenty-seven miles from Santa Barbara, Cal., is now attracting considerable attention. The reason attributed for such is the establishing of a Monte Carlo or united gambling place. The buildings will cost upwards of seven million dollars and is backed by Mexican capital. The Earp brothers are also to be interested and have full swing. The island is in sight of Santa Barbara.

*   *   *

EARP'S HALL

Early in 1894 Virgil and Allie Earp went to the gold camp at Vanderbilt, in northern San Bernardino County inland from Needles, where Virgil operated the largest saloon in town, ran unsuccessfully for local constable, and left late in the year as the boom collapsed. All of the following notes are from the Vanderbilt news columns in the Needles Eye.

August 18, 1894.

Saturday evening the sporting fraternity of this place were out in full force to witness a glove contest—a fight to a finish—between Hank Lorraine, a well-known boxer and athlete on the coast, and a colored man named John Lee, champion of Northern Arizona. The mill took place in Earp's hall, a twenty-foot ring being made in one corner and everything arranged for the convenience of participants and spectators. About 100 persons were present. Virgil W. Earp acted as referee and young Dr. Booth and Dave Congdon acted as time-keepers. Andy McShane officiated as best man for Lee.

155

October 9, 1894.

Virgil Earp is remodelling the inside of his saloon and says he will soon have a metropolitan establishment. He has also put on an addition to the rear.

December 29, 1894.

The S. M. S. gave an entertainment in Earp's hall on the 15th inst. It was well attended and everyone enjoyed themselves. A dance was given after the entertainment.

A grand ball will be held in Earp's hall Christmas eve.

Virgil Earp has sold his building, comprising saloon, public hall and dwelling, to Brown and Thompson, presumably for Charley Smithson.

*   *   *

Virgil's law enforcement plans evaporated in Vanderbilt, as the political lineup favored the Democrats. The Vanderbilt Township results are from the Needles Eye, November 6, 1894.

CONSTABLES--

V. W. Earp, R	26
F. Keyes, D. and R.	166
E. C. McNail, D.	15
A. Hamstadt, Ind.	121

*   *   *

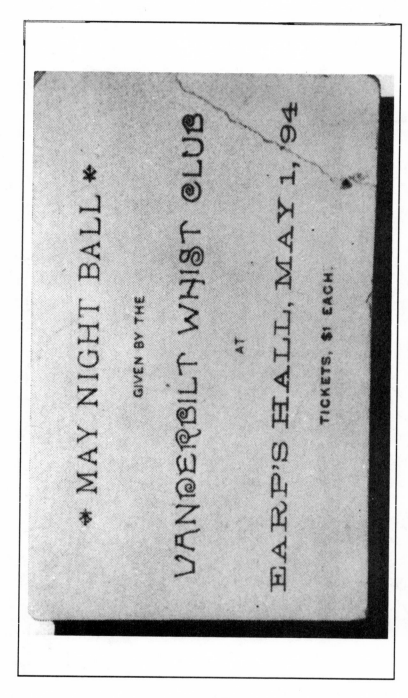

* MAY NIGHT BALL *

GIVEN BY THE

VANDERBILT WHIST CLUB

AT

EARP'S HALL, MAY 1, '94

TICKETS, $1 EACH.

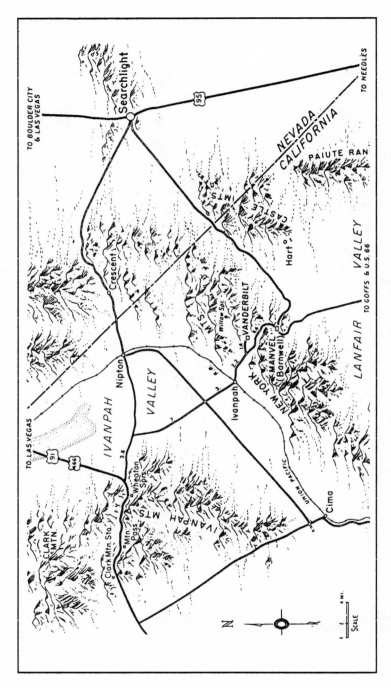

Virgil's path to the new mining camp of Vanderbilt in 1894 took him to the middle of nowhere, in one of the most rugged, hot places in California. Desert Magazine, July, 1957

O. J. Fisk knew Virgil in Vanderbilt, and in San Bernardino, and has left impressions of him; from San Bernardino Sun, April 17, 1957.

Fisk, who came to the county in 1892, often saw Wyatt Earp, whom he describes as:

"Quiet and wouldn't talk much about himself. But, yes, he was a cheerful and agreeable man. In appearance, to me, he even looked kind of studious, but he always took part in the dances and get-togethers they had in those days."

Fisk knew Virgil Earp best, since he settled in the old mining town of Vanderbilt on his arrival when Earp was running Earp's hall, a two-story saloon with a public hall upstairs.

"I was about 19 years old at the time," Fisk reminisces. "In those days there wasn't much to do but hang out around the saloon in those towns when you weren't working. I got to know Virgil pretty well.

"He was a pretty nice, gentlemanly sort of fellow. I liked him very much. . . .Fisk remembers clearly Virgil Earp's injured left arm, the elbow of which he says stopped a round of shot during a gun battle in Tombstone when Virgil was Wyatt's chief deputy.

Fisk renewed his acquaintance with Virgil Earp when he moved to San Bernardino. But the old Earp's Hall in Vanderbilt is uppermost in his memory as a busy place where there was always something going on. In the public hall upstairs, attractions ranged from dances and prizefights to church on Sundays.

*　　*　　*

TINKERING WITH THE IMAGE

Wyatt, or Wyatt working with a ghost writer, wrote a

series of articles in the San Francisco Examiner in August of 1896. The articles have been reprinted several times. Following, from the first in the series, that of August 6, are a few sentences, just to establish that Wyatt intended to upgrade, to glorify his role in several incidents.

And so I marshal my characters. My stalwart brothers, Virgil and Morgan, shall stand on the right of the stage with my dear old comrade, Doc Holliday; on the left shall be arrayed Ike Clanton, Sheriff Behan, Curley Bill and the rest. . . .But as luck would have it I stopped at Prescott to see my brother Virgil and while there I met C. P. Dake, the United States Marshal of the Territory. Dake had heard of me before, and he begged me so hard to take the deputyship in Tombstone that I finally consented. It was thus that the real troubles of a lifetime began.

*   *   *

One of the most controversial boxing bouts in U. S. history took place in San Francisco in 1896 between Jack Sharkey and Bob Fitzsimmons. Wyatt Earp was the referee, was arrested for carrying a pistol, and was criticized for how he handled the match. There is considerable literature on the bout, but the following, from the Los Angeles Times of December 5, 1896, gives Wyatt's point of view.

Wyatt Earp, the most talked-of-man of the hour, takes a philosophical view of the criticisms that are being heaped upon him for his decision on Wednesday night, and says that he will wait for time to set him right with the public.

"If I had any fears that I erred in my decision they would have disappeared when I saw Sharkey today," he said last night.

160

In the famous Fitzsimmons-Sharkey boxing match in San Francisco in 1896, Referee Wyatt Earp was criticized for toting a handgun. San Francisco Chronicle, January 2, 1927

161

"Sharkey did not strike a foul blow, to my mind. At the break he struck Fitzsimmon as soon as his arm was free, but that is following Queensbury rules. It is true that it was agreed that there was to be no fighting at the break, but my instructions from the club were not to be technical, but to give the audience a good fight for their money.

"I have one regret about the whole matter, and that is that I did not leave the ring when Julian objected to me. I thought of doing it, but it occurred to me that it would be "showing the yellow" to do that. I would be quitting under fire, and I made up my mind to stay until ordered off by the club. I am sorry that I acted as referee at all."

The only inconvenience Fitzsimmons is suffering as a result of his meeting with the sailor is a painful swelling of the joints of the hands.

"I have nothing more to say in explanation," he [Fitzsimmons] said, "except that we for a certainty know what we only surmised yesterday, and that is that members of the National Club were in this deal with Lynch and Sharkey to rob us, and what is more, we are going to prove it in court.

"Had it not been that I was saving my hands as much as possible I would have put Sharkey out in the second round. His head is as hard as a bullet, and I must have landed on him there fully forty times."

*　　*　　*

Sporting man Wyatt could not stay away from boxing matches, faro tables, or horse races. In March of 1897 he joined the thousands of fans from throughout the country who gathered in Carson City, Nevada, for the Fitzsimmons-

Corbett. His buddy Bat Masterson took the train from New York, and Wyatt went up from Los Angeles. The following is an excerpt from the Los Angeles Times of March 16, 1897.

With the crowd of common people drawn here to witness the big event on Wednesday came some of the brilliant meteors of the pugilistic world. Sharkey, arrayed in all the glory of a new broadcloth suit, was on the train and stepped off onto the platform with Dan Lynch and Wyatt Earp on either side of him. Earp looked as modest and unassuming as ever, with the same old suspicious bulge in his coat tails, and the same smile of self-satisfaction on his countenance.

* * *

Wyatt's sporting-man image and reminders of his vendetta in Arizona did not lead to a positive press in the Territory; from a news clipping, April 24, 1897, Arizona State Library.

Wyatt Earp, an old time Arizonan whose headquarters were Tombstone in the early eighties, has been sojourning at Yuma for the past few weeks: Wyatt was the associate of Doc Holliday and his gang, and was one of the principals in the Clanton-Earp feud. He was considered an all-round tough citizen and Arizona is well rid of him.

* * *

NEWTON THE GOOD

Newton, the first-born son of Nicholas Earp, was the

163

only male by the first wife. He was, then, a half-brother to the "fighting Earps," was a few years older than they, and was not closely associated with them after the 1870s. Here is a summary of Newton's particulars, provided by the Wyatt Earp Birthplace Museum, Monmouth, Illinois.

Newton Jasper Earp - Born July 10, 1837. He married Nancy Jane Adams Sept. 15, 1865. She was born in 1840. They had five children:

1. Effie May Earp - Born May 6, 1870. She married Elias Erdman, Dec. 25, 1886. She died March 29, 1898.

2. Wyatt Clyde Earp - Born August 25, 1872.

3. Mary Elizabeth Earp - Born August 25, 1875.

4. Alice Abigail Earp - Born Dec. 18, 1878. She Married Warren E. Hurt in Oct. 1896. They had one daughter, Jean May Hurt - Born Aug. 19, 1897, in Rawlins, Wyoming. She married Frank S. McKenzie July 28, 1927, in Sacramento, Calif.

5. Virgil Edwin Earp - Born April 19, 1880. ($64,000 quiz show on TV).Newton Jasper Earp died 12-25-1886 (Actually, died near Sacramento, December 18, 1929.) Nancy Adams Earp died Mar. 29, 1898.

*　　*　　*

WARREN THE IRASCIBLE

Warren Earp spent a hectic lifetime trying to earn the kind of tough reputation held by brothers Virgil and Wyatt. The following accounts illustrate the types of events that marked Warren's troubled life.

Los Angeles Herald, May 24, 1883.

It is reported that there was a shooting affair at San Bernardino on Tuesday between Warren Earp and a Mexican. Earp declined to be arrested as he acted in self defense.

Riverside Morning Enterprise, October 30, 1891.

A report reached this city last even that Warren Earp, formerly of this city, had shot and killed the City Marshal of San Jacinto. The telegraph was at once brought into requisition and it was learned that the report was a canard, as no shooting of any kind had occurred in San Jacinto.

San Bernardino Weekly Chronicle, November 26, 1892.

Last night in the M. and O. saloon on Third Street, a Mexican named Juan Bustamente and Warren Earp engaged in the pleasant pastime of cracking each other's heads. Earp got a blow on the nose which peeled that useful member somewhat, and Bustamente received a blow from a stick of wood on the side of the head, butting and bruising him slightly. Another Mexican whose name was not learned figured slightly in the fracas. Earp and Bustamente both gave bail for their appearance this morning, but the third man laid out the night in the city bastille. Two sore heads is all there was left of the difficulty.

San Bernardino Kaleidescope, August 19, 1893.

Warren Earp and Charles Steele had a fight last Monday, when

Earp cut Steele with a pocket-knife. At the trial there being no prosecuting witnesses Earp was discharged.

Clipping, Sharlot Hall Museum, Prescott, dated November 10, 1893.

Yuma, November 10. As Professor Behrens was coming from dinner he met Warren Earp, who invited him to take a walk with him across the railroad bridge, which he did. When well on the bridge he seized the professor by the throat and attempted to throw him off the bridge, but he clung to Earp and resisted till Earp said: "Give me one hundred dollars." The Professor Said, "No." "Then fifty," when he said "No." "Then twenty-five," when the professor said, "Yes, to-night."

Earp said, "I came here to kill you and throw you into the river." Both returned to town, when Behrens swore out a warrant and had Earp arrested. He is now in jail in default of bail. Earp is the youngest of the Earp brothers who made Tombstone famous in its early days.

Clipping, Sharlot Hall Museum, August 27, 1894.

Warren Earp had his examination before Judge Duke last Saturday afternoon. Upon request of the prosecuting witness he was discharged upon the charge of assault with attempt to murder. The question of the jurisdiction of the court in the case also entered into the decision as it was shown that the deed was committed 24 feet north of the middle of the bridge, and therefore in the State of California, providing the line of that state reaches to the middle of the river. Upon the charge of extortion he was placed under $250 bonds, as that part of his work was done on main street. The charge of disturbing the peace still hangs over

Warren Earp, who courted and found an early death. Colton
Public Library

him. He promised he would leave town on the first train, which he did, on Saturday evening's eastbound express. No man has left Yuma for years who was more pleased to get away. While in jail he was most penitent, and said it was the last time that he would ever get into trouble over a woman.

Warren Earp was killed in a bar in Willcox, Arizona, on July 6, 1900. The coroner's inquest, held the same day, contained several accounts, which are in the Superior Court Records of Cochise County. The following is the testimony of H. Brown, owner of the saloon.

Between one and two o'clock this morning, July 6th, 1900, [John] Boyett and deceased came into my saloon at Willcox A. T. together and commenced wrangling together near the stove. Deceased told Boyett to go and get his gun. This was the first remark I noticed particularly. Boyett left the saloon by the front door and deceased left by the rear door which connects the saloon with the restaurant. In about five minutes Boyett returned to the saloon through the front door and said: "Where is he?" He advanced to about the center of the saloon. At this time deceased was standing in the restaurant, looking through the doorway into the saloon, about one-half of his body being visible. At this instant Boyett halted about in the center of the saloon and fired two shots. After the two shots were fired, deceased stepped out on the sidewalk through a side door leading from the restaurant to the street. Boyett then stepped backwards toward the front door and fired two shots through the floor of the saloon near the stove. Deceased then stepped into the saloon through the side door of the saloon near the rear end of the saloon and advanced toward Boyett, he, deceased, opened his coat and vest and said: "I have not got any arm. You have a good deal the best of this." Deceased kept advancing toward Boyett and talking to him when Boyett told him to stop two or three times. The last time he told deceased not to come an inch closer. Boyett then fired the fifth shot. Deceased then fell to the floor face downward. Deceased never spoke after he was shot. When Boyett fired the last shot they were both standing in the front of the saloon. Did not see deceased have any gun or arms on his person at any time during the trouble.

Testimony of O. W. Hayes.

About half past one o'clock this morning, July 6, 1900, I was in Brown's saloon in Willcox, Arizona, playing a game of cards when deceased and John Boyett came in together and came up to the table where I was playing. They had a few words but I do not remember exactly what they said, only I heard deceased say to Boyett, "You was paid one hundred and fifty dollars at one time to kill me." Boyett says to deceased "I do not want to have any trouble with you." Deceased replied "Go and get your gun. I have got mine." John Boyett replied "I am not afraid of you." Boyett then left the saloon going out one door and deceased left by another door. About ten minutes afterwards Boyett came back into the saloon with two six shooters, one in each hand, and said "Where is the son-of-a-bitch". In about four or five minutes deceased came up to the door connecting the saloon and the restaurant. Then Boyett fired two shots at the deceased. I left the saloon and saw nothing more. When deceased came to the door I did not see that he was armed. When Boyett fired at deceased they were thirty-five or forty feet apart. Boyett was standing near the center of the saloon when he fired and when I left.

*　　*　　*

169

Warren's bizarre death was puzzling, as the following two newspaper accounts indicate.

Willcox Arizona Range News, July 11, 1900.

Warren Earp was shot and instantly killed by John Boyett at 1:30 Friday morning at the Headquarter saloon. It was the culmination of an ill feeling which had existed between the two men for a number of years. From evidence given at the preliminary hearing last Saturday it developed that their last quarrel began in the restaurant in the rear of the saloon. Both men came into the saloon and Earp told Boyett that he (Boyett) had been offered $100 to $150 by parties in town here to kill him. Boyett denies this and told Earp that he did not want any trouble, but added that if he had to fight him that he was not afraid. Earp told Boyett to go and get his gun, and said that he was fixed. . . .

Boyett thereupon went back to the saloon, entering at the front door and wanted to know where Earp was. Earp entered through the rear door and Boyett fired two shots at him, Earp disappeared through the same door he had entered; then he went from the restaurant through a side door out on the side walk and in a few minutes entered the saloon again through a side door. He advanced towards Boyett. Opening his coat he said: "You have the best of this, I have no gun," Boyett told him repeatedly not to advance or he would shoot. Earp still kept advancing and Boyett backed off towards the front door. Finally Boyett again repeated his warning not to advance another inch or he would shoot. Earp not heeding, Boyett fired, and Earp dropped dead.

Clipping, Sharlot Hall Museum.

Yesterday a killing occurred in Willcox which had some of the aspects of a suicide. There had been bad blood between Warren Earp and Johnny Boyett for some years. Earp had a disagreeable habit when under the influence of liquor of running Boyett all over town. Boyett, it seems, never sought a quarrel and always sought to avoid Earp when he was looking for trouble.

It was not long ago that Earp got Boyett in a saloon, and with a six-shooter pressed to his stomach, made him promise that if he and Earp ever had another quarrel a killing would result.

*   *   *

Needless to say, Warren's death was bandied about the West. Earps, by now, were press fodder. That does not mean that the reporting was accurate or objective. The Seattle Post-Intelligencer of July 22, 1900, published a three-column article on the subject, and got just about every detail confused--name of the deceased, reason for, and so forth. Following are the absurd opening sentences.

News has come that Virgil Earp, of the Earp brothers, was killed in a saloon at Wilcox, Ariz. July 7, making the third of that famous or rather notorious quartette to meet death in his ordinary foot gear, after the traditional manner of the Western bad man. And a bad man was Virgil Earp. So were all the other Earps. It was their chosen profession and they were all living exemplifications of the old adage that informs the ambitious youth that there is room at the top. For of the top rung of the ladder of this chosen profession of theirs they held full possession. Not always undisputed possession, it is true, but those who were disposed to argue the point usually came to grief in the form of the manner of death above mentioned.

There were seven of the Earps, the best known of whom were

Virgil, Wyatt, Warren and Julian, forming the quartette referred to. All of them were gunfighters and men of prompt and bitter courage. Wyatt Earp is credited with ten men, one of them his own brother-in-law.

* * *

In 1894, Nicholas and Virgil Earp registered as voters in San Bernardino County. Their particulars follow, as recorded in the Great Register entry, Colton Public Library.

REGISTER NUMBER	1439
Name	Earp, Nicholas Porter
Age	81
Height	5' 9"
Complexion	Light
Eyes	Blue
Hair	Gray
Marks or scars	None
Occupation	Farmer
Born	North Carolina
Residence	Mt. Vernon
P.O. Box	San Bernardino
Registered	26 July 1894

REGISTER NUMBER	1440
Name	Earp, Virgil W.
Age	51
Height	6' 1"
Complexion	Light
Eyes	Blue-gray
Hair	Light brown

Marks or scars	Left arm crippled
Occupation	Merchant
Born	Kentucky
Residence	Vanderbilt
P.O. Box	Vanderbilt
Registered	26 July 1894

*   *   *

QUIET IN PRESCOTT

In 1895, Virgil and Allie decided to return to Prescott and Yavapai County, where they had spent several pleasant years. The following accounts indicate some of Virgil's activities after his return.

Arizona Journal-Miner, October 23, 1895.

Virgil Earp, an old time resident of Prescott, and one of the historical characters of the territory, arrived here last evening with a view of locating here again. He came direct from Cripple Creek, Colorado. Mr. Earp will be remembered by all old timers in Prescott for the part he took, as a deputy sheriff under Ed. Bowers, in the fight which took place south of town in which two cowboys were killed. In later years Mr. Earp and his brothers figured prominently as officers at Tombstone in ridding that community of outlaws.

Clipping, Sharlot Hall Museum, November 18, 1896.

Quite a serious accident occurred yesterday at the Grizzly mine, owned by W. C. Hanson. While Virgil Earp and W. H. Harlan were working in a tunnel the ground caved, catching Mr. Earp and pinning him to the ground. He was unconscious for several hours and Dr. Abbott was called to dress his wounds, when it was discovered that his right hip was dislocated, both feet and ankles were badly crushed and his head was badly cut, besides a number of bruises on his body. The doctor says it will be several weeks before he will be able to be around.

Clipping, Sharlot Hall Museum, January 27, 1897.

Virgil Earp has recovered from the effect of his recent accident sufficiently to be able to be around on crutches. His feet were both badly mashed, his hip injured and he was bruised all over, remaining unconscious for several hours after the accident occurred. Mr. Earp has had two or three experiences in his life which very few men would have lived through, this being one of them. He has been shot all to pieces, and crushed in this mine accident, but still has hopes as well as good prospects of living to a ripe old age.

Clipping, Sharlot Hall Museum, October 25, 1898.

Mr. and Mrs. V. W. Earp have moved in from the Kirkland Valley to spend the winter in Prescott. Mr. Earp has lived and traveled all over the west and says there is no country equal to Arizona.

*   *   *

Virgil served as an officer of the courts in Yavapai County, especially as a constable. The following clippings

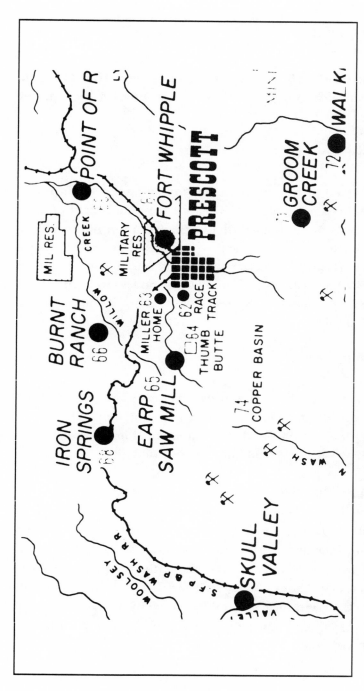

This map of historic sites near Prescott implies that the Virgil Earp saw mill enterprise was greater than it was. In the late 1870s, Virgil sawed some wood, raised a few animals, kept a hired band, but mostly drove a stage. Arizoniana, Winter, 1963

from November, 1898, are from the Sharlot Hall Museum
and indicate how Virgil got involved in a weird legal paper
hassle.

November 4.

There was a procedure yesterday involving the arrest of two
Jerome editors and a man named Lawrence on a charge of libel,
which is probably somewhat of a horseplay. John Burns, republican candidate for sheriff, swore out the warrant in Justice
Moore's court, Justice Moore appointed Virgil Earp a special
constable and Mr. Earp hied him over the taxless to Jerome with
his warrant. He nabbed Lawrence and James Thompson and
brought them in last evening.

November 5.

Virgil Earp was arrested Saturday evening and brought before
Justice Campbell on a charge of false imprisonment. The justice
placed Earp under $500 bond to appear before him for preliminary
examination. Earp gave bail and was released.

November 6.

Most any ordinary fool knows that a justice of the peace has
authority to issue a warrant and to deputize anyone to serve it.
There is, however, an occasional democratic fool that don't even
know that much. The arrest of Virgil Earp for false imprisonment,
charged with serving a warrant duly issued by a peace officer of
the county, proves the allegation that some fools don't know as
much as an ordinary clam.

176

*   *   *

Virgil Earp had three wives, and this article from the Portland Oregonian of April 22, 1899, clarifies some of the marriage history.

Virgil W. Earp, brother of Wyatt Earp, of Sharkey-Fitzsimmons fight fame, and a man with a record of his own, is in Portland enjoying a reunion with this first wife and his only daughter, neither of whom he has seen for 39 years. The wife is now the widow of the late Thomas Eaton, and Earp has another at Prescott, Ariz. The story of the separation is one of those romances which give color to the adage that truth once in a while is stranger than fiction.

Earp was married to his first wife, then Ellen Rysdam, at Oakaloosa, Ia., in February, 1860. He was then 17 years old and she was still younger. The parents of both young people strenuously opposed the match—the girl's parents because they did not want their daughter, who was a native of Holland, to marry into an American family; Earp's because he was too young. So the wedding was kept secret, the couple got only an occasional opportunity to see each other, and not till the birth of their daughter did they make their union known. Then there was trouble on both sides of the house, which, however, was soon stilled by the enlistment of Earp in the civil war, when his child was two weeks old, and his immediate departure for the front.

His young wife was left with her parents, who continually urged her to secure a divorce from her husband, and who finally took it upon themselves to declare the union at an end. Soon word was received that Earp was wounded, then that he was dead, and his wife had no reason to doubt either report. With her parents she came West, bringing her child, and in 1867 she married Thomas

Eaton at Walla Walla.

In the meantime Earp returned to his home, found his wife gone, heard from friends that she had married again, and philosophically decided that the best thing he could do was to keep out of her way.

This he did very successfully. He married again in 1873, came West, and took an active part in the stirring times on the plains that have furnished unlimited inspiration for Old Sleuth and other chroniclers of cowboy days. He was the famous chief of police of Tombstone, at the time of the killing of "Doc" Halliday. His brother Wyatt, "Bat" Masterson, and other characters whose names have filled the blaring trumpet of fame were there at that time and took a hand in what happened. Earp carries a lame arm which was plugged full of lead, and can tell many reminiscences that affect the hair like a stiff sea breeze.

All this time Mrs. Eaton was busy rearing a family of five children, the eldest of whom was Earp's daughter, Janie, now Mrs. Levi Law. She came to Portland about 19 years ago, and for a long time has lived on North Front street, opposite the United States engineers' mooring ground. Her husband, who was a well known wood dealer, died several years ago. After a while she heard that there was nothing in the story about Earp's death, but under the circumstances she was not especially eager to renew the acquaintance. Even when she found that he had been keeping himself informed in a general way of her welfare and that of his daughter, there was no correspondence. Earp, having the second Mrs. Earp to care for, made no effort to restore the first wife to his fireside. Had circumstances been such that this was entirely agreeable, he was not at all sure that she still cared for him.

The present reunion was brought about by the recent illness of Earp's daughter, Mrs. Law, who had learned the story of her father and discovered that his present residence was at Prescott,

178

VIRGIL EARP—HIS LONG-LOST WIFE AND THEIR DAUGHTER.

Portland Oregonian, April 22, 1899

Ariz. She had been corresponding with him since September, and expected to make him a visit last winter, but a sudden attack of pneumonia changed her plans, and instead her father hastened to her bedside.

He is now enjoying a very pleasant visit with her and his two grandchildren, at her home, which is near that of Mrs. Eaton, in North Portland. He will remain for several days more, before he starts on his journey home. Years have taken away the pain the meeting between the former husband and wife would once have caused, and the little visit has been a most happy one for all.

*   *   *

A letter from George Bertrand, dated October 21, 1958, appears in Turner's The Earps Talk. Bertrand's grandfather had married Virgil Earp's granddaughter, and he offered the following insight into the unusual marriage and separation.

Ellen Rysdam and Virgil Earp had been keeping company for quite some time when they decided to marry. Ellen's folks when approached about it, flew into a rage and forbid her to marry below her station in life. They also insisted that they stop their courtship and to never see each other again. Of course this merely threw them together close and the first time that they could slip away, they did so. Their marriage was made in secret in one of the adjoining counties and then kept secret until such time as when she became pregnant. At the same time, the Civil War broke out and to escape the wrath of her father, Virgil joined the service with his brothers or brother. Father Rysdam tried to have the marriage annulled but because he couldn't find out where they had been married failed. This being due to the fact that Ellen refused to tell him where they were married. When Virgil's efforts to contact Ellen by mail came into being, again Father Rysdam interfered. Then someone returned form the front and told the story that Virgil had died in one of the training camps and that he had seen him buried. Of course this brought about the opportunity for Father Rysdam to step in and insist on the marriage of his choice. The Van Rossen marriage. Ellen and her child soon became Van Rossens whereupon they then started out west.

*   *   *

Land Claim, copy in Archives, Sharlot Hall Museum.

NOTICE FOR PUBLICATION, Land Office at Prescott, Arizona, March 6, 1900. Notice is hereby given that the following named settler has filed notice of his intention to make final proof in support of his claim, and that said proof will be made before the Register and Receiver at Prescott, Ariz., on Wednesday, April 11, 1900, viz: Virgil W. Earp, H. E. 1449, for the SW 1/4, of SE 1/4, of sec 17 and N 1/2 of NE 1/4, and SE 1/4 of NE 1/4, of sec. 20, twp 12, N R 4 W.

He names the following witnesses to prove his continuous residence upon, and cultivation of said land, viz:

William Rudy, T. M. Earnhart, James More, Mose Langley, all of Kirkland, Ariz.

FREDERICK A. TRITLE, JR., Register

*   *   *

Virgil decided to get back in law enforcement, and at the

1900 Republican Convention in Yavapai County was a teller and election official. The following notes appeared in the Arizona Weekly Journal-Miner.

September 26, 1900.

For sheriff Judge E. W. Wells placed the name of Virgil Earp before the convention and he was nominated by acclamation.

October 3, 1900.

Virgil Earp has withdrawn as candidate for sheriff on the Republican ticket. The position on the ticket will be left vacant.

*   *   *

Virgil Earp has left few samples of bad judgement or distortion in his wake. However, when he accepted the nomination for sheriff of Yavapai County, he concocted a new history for himself during the Dodge City days, but stayed close to the facts concerning Prescott and Tombstone; from Arizona Republican, September 26, 1900.

Virgil Earp was nominated for sheriff by acclamation, by the Republican Convention at Prescott last Saturday. At the ratification meeting held in the evening by the McKinley-Roosevelt Club, candidates were present and expressed themselves.

Earp was called upon and made one of the best speeches of the evening. "No doubt," he said, "many of you have heard of me. I want to tell you a few things. In 1874 I went to Dodge City, and I tell you boys, she was the wildest town on the American

182

Continent. I had been there only a short time when business men and property owners came to me and said, 'Earp, you must help us to overcome the lawlessness in this city.' I replied, 'I don't want it, give it to someone else.' They said, 'If you don't take the city marshalship we will have to leave town.' So in the interest of law and order I accepted, and I leave it to the law-abiding citizens of Dodge City as to whether I performed my duty or not. . . .

*   *   *

FROM DESERT TO ICE FLOW

The gold fever in the Klondike and at Nome affected Wyatt, and he and Josephine spent several years in Alaska, mostly at Nome, earning gold pieces by pushing drinks and poker. The following notes indicate how Wyatt was spending his time.

Undated clipping, Alaska State Museum, Juneau.

A POPULAR ESTABLISHMENT OF NOME. In this issue will be found an [a drawing] of Cape Nome, who never had a lesson in drawing in his life. This property, which is one of the most valuable and largest business blocks in the town of Nome, is owned and occupied by Wyatt Earp and C. E. Hoxsie, who, as partners, conduct the Dexter Saloon and club rooms therein. The upper portion of the building is occupied by professional men for offices. The Dexter is 30 x 70, with 12-foot ceilings. It is neatly and handsomely equipped and furnished, and enjoys a literal patronage from the people of Nome. . . .Mr. Earp is now "outside" purchasing the stock.

183

Alaska State Museum

Contrary to many reports, Wyatt did not run Alaska's only "Second Class Saloon." As can be seen here, he was proud of his "First Class Stock." Nome Gold Digger, August 15, 1900

Nome Gold Digger, October 25, 1899.

Wyatt Earp, who was Deputy U. S. Marshal in Arizona at one time, and who is a celebrated personage in nearly all the mining camps of the country, left on the steamer Cleveland for San Francisco.

Nome Daily News, June 29, 1900.

A STREET BRAWL. Some little excitement was occasioned on Front street this morning by the occurrence of a drunken row. The fracas was commenced by Dan Kane and E. P. Lopez, both of whom were intoxicated. Kane threatened the life of Lopez and the former was placed under arrest by Deputy Marshals Quinlan and Gunn. As the officers were conducting their prisoner towards the barracks, several persons interfered and Kane's release was forcibly effected. At this juncture, Deputy Marshal Lowe arrived upon the scene, and with his assistance Kane was apprehended a second time. Wyatt Earp was likewise taken into custody; he is charged with interfering with an officer while in the discharge of his duty. Kane is now confined in jail. Earp, upon reaching the barracks, asserted that his action had been misconstrued, and that he had interceded to assist the deputy marshal. Commissioner Shepard released Earp on his own recognizance. The Cases will come up before Commissioner Swinehart sometime tomorrow.

Nome Daily News, September 12, 1900.

COMMISSIONER'S COURT. The principals in a fracas which occurred in the Dexter Saloon, were arraigned before Commissioner Stevens this morning. The accused parties were Wyatt Earp, N. Marcus (Wyatt's brother-in-law) and Walter Summers. About 12 o'clock last night Patrolman Vanslow of the U. S. A. arrested Summers for disorderly conduct. The soldier, while performing this duty, was assaulted and beaten by Wyatt Earp and N. Marcus. The latter is a porter in the Dexter Saloon. Assistance was rendered to the officer, and eventually the apprehension of Summers, Earp and Marcus was effected. Summers, at a trial this morning, established his innocence, and he was accordingly discharged. The cases against the other two prisoners were continued at 2 o'clock tomorrow afternoon, and in the meantime the defendants are at liberty upon cash bonds of $20 each.

*　　*　　*

Robert H. "Bob" Paul had one of the longest law enforcement careers in the West, beginning as deputy sheriff in Calaveras County, California, in 1858. He was closely linked with the Earp faction in Arizona, where he

A meeting on the golden sands of Nome in 1900. Wyatt is in the center, and to the right is ex-Tombstone Mayor John Clum. To the left is Ed Englestadt, a local gold miner whose partner Charles Hoxsie ran the Dexter Saloon with Wyatt. Alaska State Museum

served as sheriff of Pima County and as a Deputy U. S. Marshal. The following is from his obituary, provided by the Wells, Fargo History Room, San Francisco.

Robert H. Paul, who for the past thirty years has been an officer in California and Arizona, died at Tucson, Ariz., March 26th. He was one of the most interesting characters in Arizona, and his life work embraced many daring deeds, chief among them being the breaking up of the notorious Tom Bell gang of desperadoes, who operated in California in early days. Coming to Arizona, Paul was engaged as "shotgun" messenger for Wells, Fargo & Co., guarding the stage between Tucson and Tombstone. He had many thrilling experiences while serving in that capacity, and it was he who secured the services of the famous Earp boys for service as Wells, Fargo & Co. guards.

*   *   *

Wyatt returned from Alaska to Los Angeles for a visit in late 1901. He was interviewed by the Los Angeles Times, December 12, 1901.

Wyatt Earp, the well-known sporting authority, passed the day in Los Angeles with his wife. He has just returned from Nome, where he has mining properties sufficient to make him financially comfortable for the remainder of his life. He states that the inland prospects at Nome are proving rich and that practical miners, who apply themselves steadily, are taking out good money.

Mr. Earp has not retired from the world of sport. He states that he intends to enjoy the roped arena and other characteristic sports for some time yet, although the criticism he received from his decision in the Sharkey-Fitzsimmons fight was unfair, he alleges.

"I easily can explain the attack of certain newspapers," said

Mr. Earp. "I had been doing work for the Examiner for three months previous to the fight. At that time both the Call and Chronicle were bitterly fighting the Examiner, and when I refereed the mill, I was their chance to get back at their rival over me. However, a referee is always open to the attacks of newspapers, friends of either fighter and to incompetent sporting editors who have exalted opinions of themselves."

Mr. and Mrs. Earp will continue their journey south tomorrow and will return to Nome the coming season.

*   *   *

ICE FLOW TO DESERT

Wyatt and Josie left the frozen beaches of Nome for the desert promise of Nevada. The following newspaper comment is from the Tonopah Bonanza of February 1, 1902.

Wyatt Earp and wife and H. Martin arrived from Los Angeles Tuesday. Mr. Earp has just returned from Nome and came to Tonopah to engage in the saloon business. He had a big wagon loaded down with software and as soon as he and his partner Mr. Martin secure a location they will be home to all. They are good citizens and we welcome them to Tonopah.

*   *   *

The following, on file in the Print Collection, Nevada Historical Society, is an example of Wyatt Earp's long association with law enforcement.

IN THE CIRCUIT COURT OF THE UNITED STATES, NINTH CIRCUIT, DISTRICT OF NEVADA. C. C. Eisle Plaintiff, vs. T. L.

189

Oddie, Frank Butler, A. H. Bass, W. W. Booth, John Doe & Richard Roe, defendants. I certify and return that I received the within and hereto annexed SUMMONS at Tonopah, Nevada, on the 22nd day of June, 1902, and that I personally served the same upon the defendants therein named, T. L. Oddie, A., H. Bass and W. W. Booth at Tonopah, Nye County, Nevada, on the 23rd day of June, 1902, and upon Frank Butler at Tonopah, Nevada, on the 24th day of June, 1902, by exhibiting the said annexed Summons to each of them at the times and place above mentioned, and leaving in possession of each of them a copy of the said Summons, attached to a certified copy of the complaint; the said certified copies being certified to be the Clerk of the above entitled court, as being full, true and correct copies of the original complaint now on file in his office in the above entitled case.

I further return that the said defendants, John Doe and Richard Roe are parties unknown to me.

Dated: Tonopah, Nevada   /s/J. F. Emmitt
June 29, 1902   U. S. Marshal
MEMORANDA OF FEES   /s/ Wyatt Earp
4 Services-----$16.00   Deputy U. S. Marshal,
    District of Nevada

*　　*　　*

Tonopah Miner, June 26, 1902, both items.

James C. Earp, brother of Wyatt Earp of the Northern, came in from San Francisco Monday evening.

FORMERLY IN ALASKA Wyatt Earp and George Woods ran the "Dexter" and "Cape Nome" saloons in Nome, and they are both embarked in the same business here.

190

Wyatt's Northern saloon, Tonopah was short-lived. Nevada Historical Society

*　　　*　　　*

At this stage in his career Wyatt was frequently mentioned in newspaper articles, and not all of these notices were positive. He was frequently praised, but he could not keep up with the many distorted newspapers and magazine articles. An article in the Los Angeles Herald of September 8, 1903, about Wyatt's alleged cowardice and evil ways in Alaska, prompted two replies. The first, by Wyatt, appeared in the Herald of September 8; the second, by George Whitwell Parsons, appeared in the issue of September 9.

Wyatt.

It relates to an experience I was reported to have had in Dawson City, in which I was said to have attempted to "shoot up the town" and to have been subdued by one of the Canadian Mounted Police.

The falsity of the article is shown by the fact that I never was within 1000 miles of Dawson City.

I wish to say that neither I nor my bothers were ever "bad men," in the sense that term is used, nor did we ever indulge in the practice of "shooting up" towns. We have been officers of the law and have had our experiences in preserving the law, but we are not, and never have been professional bad men. In justice to me and my friends and relatives I would like to have you make this statement.

/S/ WYATT EARP

Parsons.

As an old Tombstoner and one who knew the Earps in the stormy days of the early '80s, I wish, in simple justice to the family

192

in general and Wyatt Earp in particular, to confirm his statement in yesterday's Herald that they were not "bad men" in the common acceptation of the term, but were ever ready to discharge their duty as officers of the law, and did it so effectively that they incurred the enmity of the rustlers and desperadoes congregated in that lively town and section of the country and were always on the side of law and order.

There was one exception. When their brother Morgan was assassinated, Virgil Earp shot and Wyatt Earp's life attempted, then they took the law into their own hands and did what most anyone would have done under the peculiar circumstances existing at the time, and what anyone reading the Virginian would consider their right to do.

I speak of a time I am familiar with for I lived in Tombstone during the entire stay of the Earps, chased Apaches with them, and have seen them, and particularly Wyatt Earp, defending and enforcing the law in the face of death. To call such men "bad men," when the better element was siding with and supporting them morally and financially, is to deal is terms misapplied; and I feel today as I felt in Nome, Alaska, where I saw Wyatt Earp, that if anybody was undeservedly illtreated and particularly an old Tombstoner, he would find a champion in the same Wyatt Earp, who is older now but none the less gritty, I believe. I state this in justice to a much maligned man who, as a public character, was a benefit and a protection to the community he once lived in.

/S/ G. W. PARSONS

*   *   *

MORGAN IN THE DEEP, SOMEWHERE

After Morgan's assassination in Tombstone in 1882, his

193

body was removed to Colton, California, for burial. He may have rested in peace, but where is not known. Following, from the Colton Public Library, is a statement from the Librarian, Mrs. Jane E. MacLin, dated August 26, 1952.

Local tradition has it that Morgan's body was buried in the old cemetery at what is now the south-west corner of Rancho and Highway 99, at the western approach to Colton. When the Southern Pacific Railroad bought a right of way through this land [c. 1892] the cemetery was abandoned. Remains buried there were moved to the Hermosa Cemetery in Colton. Many graves were unmarked and remains from such graves were re-interred and listed on Hermosa Cemetery records as "unknown." There is no record of Morgan Earp's burial place and it is supposed that his original grave was unmarked and that his remains were among the re-interrments listed as "unknown."

*   *   *

A brother of Nick Earp, the Rev. J. D. Earp, remained and his family prospered in Lamar, Barton County, Missouri. His son, John M. Earp, later served as mayor of Lamar. The following are a few Earp paragraphs from the Lamar Republican, November, 1905, copy in the Colton Public Library.

Hon. John M. Earp, former mayor of the city of Lamar, is a member of the city council from the first ward, having been elected last spring. He is a recognized leader on the floor of the council, in its deliberations and in all official matters pertaining to the government of the city. He is one of the city's conscientious and scrupulous officials and citizens, who never has cast a vote detrimental to the city's interests. He has advocated certain needed reforms, has stood for economy in the disbursement of the city's limited revenues and has invariably supported such measures as deserved his vote and support.

These pointed remarks explain a great deal in Mr. Earp's official conduct. Bold, fearless, astute and shrewd, he is one of the best politicians in Southwest Missouri, but with all his political successes he has never stooped once to do a thing not consistent with the very best interests of those whom he is trying to serve.

* * *

VIRGIL'S LAST BADGE

Virgil's last call for gold, and law enforcement, was the rush to Tonopah and Goldfield in 1905. His racked body prevented him from doing any mining, but he acted as a bouncer and "special officer" at the National Club in Goldfield. He was also carrying a badge, as is indicated in this oath, in the Nevada Historical Society Archives.

OATH OF OFFICE—STATE OF NEVADA—COUNTY OF ESMERALDA

I, V. W. Earp do solemnly swear that I will support, protect and defend the Constitution and Government of the United States and the Constitution and Government of the State of Nevada, against all enemies, whether domestic or foreign, and that I will bear true faith, allegiance and loyalty to the same, any ordinance or law of any State convention or Legislature to the contrary notwithstanding, and further that I do this with a full determination, pledge and purpose, without any mental reservation or evasion whatsoever. And I do further solemnly swear that I have

195

not fought a duel, nor sent nor accepted a challenge to fight a duel, nor been a second to either party, nor in any manner aided or assisted in such duel, nor been knowingly the bearer of such challenge or acceptance, since the adoption of the Constitution of the State of Nevada, and that I will not be so engaged or concerned directly or indirectly, in or about any such duel during my continuance in office. And further that I will well and faithfully perform all the duties of the office of Deputy Sheriff on which I am about to enter so help me God.

/Virgil W Earp

Hawthorne, Nev. Jan. 26th 1905

I hereby designate and appoint V. W. Earp of Goldfield Deputy Sheriff in and for Esmeralda county, State of Nevada, during my pleasure.

/s/ J. F. Bradley

Sheriff and ex-officio Assessor, Esmeralda county, Nevada

*　　*　　*

Wyatt also decided to try the Nevada goldfields again. The Tonopah Sun of February 5, 1905, reported the following.

Verge Earp, a brother of Wyatt and one of the famous family of gunologists, is acting as deputy sheriff in the National Club, Goldfield. Verge is a mild looking individual and to outward view presents none of the characteristics that have made the family name a familiar one in the west and in all the bonanza camps of the country from Mexico to Alaska.

Wyatt is expected in Goldfield shortly. He is coming overland from Los Angeles with his wife, dog, and trusty rifle. Wyatt is no

OATH OF OFFICE.

STATE OF NEVADA, }
County of Esmeralda } ss

V. W. Earp do solemnly swear that I will support protect and defend the Constitution and Government of the United States and the Constitution and Government of the State of Nevada, against all enemies, whether domestic or foreign, and that I will bear true faith, allegiance and loyalty to the same, any ordinance or law of any State convention or Legislature to the contrary notwithstanding; and further that I do this with a full determination, pledge and purpose, without any mental reservation or evasion whatsoever. And I do further solemnly swear that I have not fought a duel, nor sent nor accepted a challenge to fight a duel, nor been a second to either party, nor in any manner aided or assisted in such duel, nor been knowingly the bearer of such challenge or acceptance, since the adoption of the Constitution of the State of Nevada, and that I will not be so engaged or concerned directly or indirectly, in or about any such duel during my continuance in office. And further that I will well and faithfully perform all the duties of the office of _Deputy Sheriff_ on which I am about to enter so help me God.

Subscribed and sworn to before me this _27th_

day of _May_ 190_5_

Louis Foucault _Virgil W Earp_
Notary Public

Hawthorne, Nev. _Jan 26th_ 1905

I hereby designate and appoint _V. W. Earp_ of _Goldfield_ Deputy Sheriff and ex-officio Assessor in and for Esmeralda county, State of Nevada. _during my pleasure_

J. F. Bradley
Sheriff and ex-officio Assessor Esmeralda county, Nevada.

Nevada Historical Society

more an exponent of quick and rapid target practice. He has forsworn the green cloth and the automatic revolver and is now dependent on his ability as a miner for a living as well as his fame. In a recent letter to his brother in Goldfield, Wyatt asserted that he would never shoot at a man again unless the man tries to shoot at me first.

The Earps have several claims in and about Bullfrog out of which they hope to make a goodly sum. They examined the vicinity of Goldfield some years ago but were not favorably impressed with what they saw, an opinion many another shared with them until two years ago. Before arriving here, Wyatt will stay in the Bullfrog country for several weeks. He expects to consume about two months on the journey from the city of the Angels. He is comfortably fitted out with tents, wagons and other paraphernalia necessary for prospector life.

*   *   *

Virgil's stay in Goldfield was short, as he died there of pneumonia on October 19, 1905. The following is a portion of the obituary from the Arizona Daily Journal-Miner, October 27, 1905.

FEARLESS RANGER SUCCUMBS TO DEATH—Demise of Virgil Earp, Early Resident of Prescott—Many An Outlaw Fell A Victim To His Rifle.

Word reached here yesterday from Goldfield, Nevada, of the death at that place of Virgil Earp on October 19, of pneumonia, and the shipment of his remains to Portland, Oregon, for burial. He was born in the state of Indiana, and was 63 years of age at the time of his death. He was one of the best known men on the Pacific coast, as well as one of the bravest.

In company with his two brothers, Wyatt and Morgan, and Doc Holliday, he came to Prescott about the year 1877. Shortly after his arrival here, and while Ed Bowers was sheriff of Yavapai county, the town was visited by two cowboys from the Bradshaw basin section, who enlivened matters by shooting up saloons and other resorts, finally riding out of the place, shooting right and left as they went in the direction of the Brooks ranch just outside the city limits.

Arriving at Brooks ranch, the cowboys sent word to the officers that they were camped there, and if any of the officers wanted them to come out and get them. These men were considered bad ones, and were known to be dead shots. Sheriff

Bowers organized a posse of citizens, of which Virgil Earp happened to be one, and the posse started for the Brooks ranch on horseback preceded by Deputy United States Marshal Stanford and another deputy in a hack. The party in the hack passed the bad men unmolested, but the cowboys opened fire on the sheriff's posse, which was on horseback. Sheriff Bowers' horse was shot in several places, but he returned the fire, and did not get hit.

On arriving at the scene Virgil Earp, who was armed with a Henry rifle, preceded up the creek in the direction of the shooting, and noticing one of the cowboys crouching under an oak tree reloading his gun, shot and killed him dead. The first shot hit him in the heart, and the second shot struck about two inches from the first. The other cowboy was shot with a charge of buckshot and lived for two days, finally dying in the hospital. . . .

About ten years ago Virgil Earp returned to the county and engaged in mining in the Hassayampa district, subsequently moving to Kirkland valley district. In the year 1900 he was nominated for sheriff by the Republican party, but shortly afterwards withdrew from the race.

During his stormy career as an officer in Tombstone he always had the support of the law abiding element of the community and from first to last was recognized as being the brains of the official combination which included himself and brothers and Doc Holliday, although all saw who were acquainted with all of them that a more fearless man never lived than Holliday, who died in Colorado two years ago from the same malady, pneumonia, which on the 19th of this month proved fatal to Virgil Earp. Holliday was considered a handsome man and was a dentist by profession.

A great many harsh things have been said and written about the "Earp gang," but nevertheless it is a fact that a more charitable man never lived than Virgil Earp, especially when he had the means to render assistance. Every desperate act ever known to

199

Goldfield, Nevada, was in its mining boom phase when Virgil Earp arrived early in 1905; he died there later in the year. Natural History Museum, Los Angeles

Goldfield street scene. Natural History Museum, Los Angeles

have been committed by him was clothed with the authority of law, and he was ever known to avoid personal encounters except when invested with legal authority and in the discharge of this duty.

*   *   *

Nick Earp died in the Soldier's Home, Sawtelle, near Los Angeles, on February 12, 1907. The following death notice, which appeared in the Los Angeles Times of February 14, was not completely accurate, but the space they gave to Nick, plus a portrait of him, indicate the significance of the Earp name in the region.

"Old Judge" Earp, frontier justice and father of the noted "Earp boys," who have figured prominently in the Southwest, and especially in Arizona and New Mexico, died in the Home hospital yesterday.

Nicholas P. Earp, who was a native of Kentucky, served during the Mexican War as sergeant in Capt. W. B. Stapp's company of Illinois Mounted Volunteers. At the close of the war he settled in Iowa and was elected justice of the peace in the then not over-populous Marion county.

When the Civil War was begun, he, at the request of the Governor of Iowa, organized troops in his county, and was appointed deputy United States provost-marshal for his Congress district; doing excellent service while in that office.

After the war he removed with his family to the Southwest and lived for a number of years in Arizona and New Mexico, and then to Colton, where he again filled the office of justice of the peace. His health failing him, he, in 1907, came to the home, where he

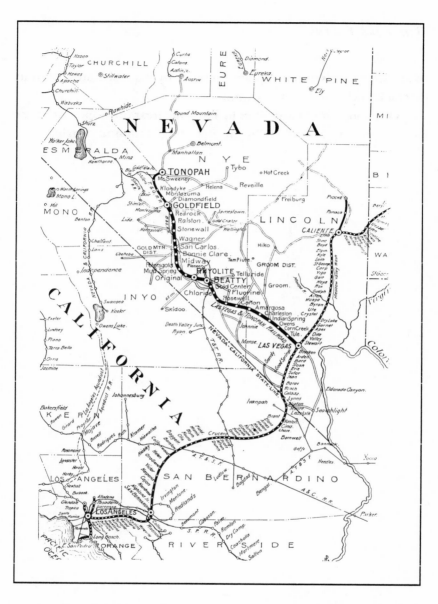

Wyatt tried the mining camp at Tonopah, and Virgil's last stop was at Goldfield in 1905. Natural History Museum, Los Angeles

203

was esteemed as an exemplary member by his associates, both in barrack and later in the hospital.

One son, James Earp, lives in Sawtelle, near the home. Another son, Nathan (Newton), is in the Searchlight mining district.

CHAPTER 4
FINE-TUNING OF LEGENDS

**In 1907, Bat Masterson published a work entitled Fa-
mous Gunfighters, and devoted a chapter to Wyatt, whom
he knew on the Kansas Plains as well as in Tombstone. Here
are a few of the opening paragraphs.**

Wyatt Earp is one of the few men I personally knew in the West
in the early days, whom I regarded as absolutely destitute of
physical fear. I have often remarked, and I am not alone in my
conclusion, that what goes for courage in a man is generally the
fear of what others will think of him—in other words, personal
bravery is largely made of self-respect, egotism, and an apprehension of the opinion of others.

Wyatt Earp's daring and apparent recklessness in time of
danger is wholly characteristic; personal fear doesn't enter into
the equation, and when everything is said and done, I believe he

William Barclay "Bat" Masterson, an "Easterner" for his last thirty years, as an author helped romanticize and exaggerate Wyatt's role in the West. Wyatt and Bat had hunted buffalo together and later were lawmen in Ford County, Kansas. Colton Public Library

values his own opinion of himself more than that of others, and it is his own good report that he seeks to preserve.

*　　*　　*

Wyatt could never stay away from the "green cloth," and this bunco incident of 1911 suggests his close familiarity with a scam, and perhaps a participation in it. The Walter Scott mentioned in the case was "Death Valley Scotty," at the beginning of his public career as folksy con-man and exaggerator.

Los Angeles Times, July 25, 1911.

CHARGE MORE SERIOUS

The charge of vagrancy made against Wyatt Earp, Walter Scott and Harry Dean, who, J. Y. Peterson, a real estate man, complained had attempted to fleece him out of a large amount of money in a game of faro Friday night, will be changed in Police Court, today to one of having conspired to conduct a gambling game. The fact that the detectives broke into the room in the Auditorium Hotel where the game had been set up, and arrested the trio before operations had begun, prevents the placing of the more serious charge, conspiracy to defraud, against them.

The charge of conspiracy as applied in the cases against the three men, is a misdemeanor and can be disposed of in Police Court.

All of the paraphernalia which was found in the room when the police broke in, is in the hands of the police. It consists of a faro layout, dealing box, a deck of cards in the center of each of which is a small hole so that the dealer can see at a glance if the second card down is odd or even, and 100 chips, such as are used in the regulation faro game.

Los Angeles Times, July 26, 1911.

WANT MORE TIME

One of the trio charged with having conspired to lift a large amount of money from J. Y. Peterson, a real estate dealer, with a "phony" faro layout could not weather the blow that overtook them in police court yesterday when they were charged with conspiracy and he is now moored inside the City Jail. It was Harry Dean who was unable to furnish $500 bail. Wyatt Earp and Walter Scott are at liberty but must appear in Police Judge Rose's court Thursday to plead.

The charge against them now is simply "conspiring to violate the law prohibiting gambling." In the mind of the city prosecutor this is the only one that can be lodged against them, because the police broke into the room before operations had begun.

The charges of vagrancy filed against the three in Police Judge Chambers's court last week will probably be dismissed when the conspiracy trial is taken up in the other police court.

Los Angeles Times, July 28, 1911.

SAY NOT GUILTY

Wyatt Earp, Walter Scott and Harry Dean, charged with conspiracy in connection with an alleged attempt to fleece J. Y. Peterson, a real estate dealer, out of $2000 in a game of faro, pleaded not guilty in Police Judge Rose's court yesterday. They will be tried September 27 and 28, two days deemed necessary for a full hearing.

After making their pleas Earp and Scott left the Police Court building while Dean appeared in Police Judge Chambers's court to plead to the charge of vagrancy which was made against them when first arrested. The men are out on $500 bail in each court.

Dean will be given a trial on the vagrancy charge August 17.

Los Angeles Times, September 28, 1911.

THEY'RE RELEASED. SPORTING MEN LET GO. Wyatt Earp and Walter Scott, were released yesterday afternoon and the charges of conspiracy against them were dismissed by Police Judge Rose. Earp, was released because the city prosecutor decided there was not sufficient evidence against him to warrant calling a jury. The prosecutor was too busy to take up Scott's trial and it was dropped.

Harry Dean of Livingston, Mont., pleaded guilty to the charge a few weeks ago, and was released under a suspended sentence of six months upon his promise to leave the city.

Scott agreed to plead guilty under assurance that he would be given a suspended sentence but yesterday changed his mind and demanded a jury trial. The prosecutor had been assured that a jury trial would not be asked and no arrangement had been made.

The trio, were charged with having conspired to run a faro bank game in the Auditorium Hotel. J. Y. Peterson, a real estate man was invited to risk his money but called the police instead.

Earp was in the room when the police entered but contended that he was not connected with the game and had simply dropped in by accident. No evidence against him was secured.

*   *   *

Wyatt spent much of the period 1910-1929 working mining claims in the Whipple Mountains. He had homes in both Vidal Junction and in the town of Earp. San Bernardino Sun-Telegram, June 25, 1961

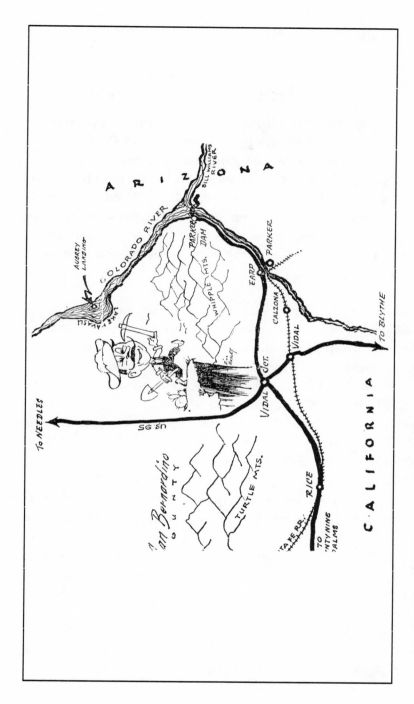

Map of Town of Earp. San Bernardino Sun-Telegram, June 25, 1961

211

BACK TO THE DESERT

In 1906, Wyatt and Josephine geared up to exploit their small copper-gold claims in San Bernardino County, near the Colorado River. A Los Angeles neighbor, Mrs. Nellie Blair, had recommended a friend to help Wyatt, John Flood, a bookkeeper who had been educated at Yale and Bucknell. Flood would become an Earp intimate for decades. Here is a portion of an interview with Flood which details some Earp activities from that early period; San Bernardino Sun-Telegram, April 22, 1956.

The Earps bought a wagonload of gear and headed south on the old Parker Road which went directly over the hills south from town and then angled southeast into Chemehuevi Valley. The first load was driven a half day's journey out of Needles and cached. Earp returned to Needles, bought a second load, and hauled it all the way to Hank's Well where a tent was erected. There Mrs. Earp stayed on guard with their dog while Earp and Flood returned to Needles for a third load. A second camp was established at West Well, which incidentally was east of Hank's Well.

The first cached load was hauled to West Well. Then the supplies from Hank's Well were hauled to the new camp. In that manner, with one wagon and a single team, the trio carried a season's provisions, camp equipment and mining tools into the Whipple Mountains. While the Earps worked developing their claims, Flood looked around and made locations both for Mrs. Blair and for himself. Mrs. Earp cooked for the two men in the tent camp.

The journey of 1906 was repeated many times though never again was it necessary to take such a multiple load trek nor drive horses all the way from Los Angeles to the Colorado.

212

Summer heat being what it is in the rocky hills that constitute the Whipples, the Earps customarily divided the year between the summer months in Los Angeles and the fall-winter spring months at the mines. The man, who had become a national hero of law enforcement in turbulent camps, became known throughout the district as an affable but somewhat shy mine proprietor who didn't like to talk about the past and shunned publicity. The Earps were solid citizens, liked by other district residents.

*   *   *

In 1912, Newton Earp applied for a pension for his Civil War service. The following information accompanied his application, which is in the National Archives.

Newton Jasper Earp
Born: Ohio County, Kentucky, October 7, 1837
Married: Nancy Jane Adam, in Marion County, Missouri, September 12, 1865, Rev. Hunt officiating; she died March 29, 1898, Paradise, Nevada
Children: Effie May, born May 6, 1870
Wiatt Clyde, born August 25, 1872
Mary Elizabeth, born August 25, 1875
Alice Abigail, born December 18, 1878
Virgil Edwin, born April 19, 1880
Description: 5' 8 1/2" tall, dark complexion, blue eyes, brown hair

*   *   *

One of the champions of the Earp brothers in the Tombstone days was Acting Governor John J. Gosper. The

213

following two excerpts indicate the heights and depths possible in a career.

Arizona Weekly Star, September 15, 1881.

Just now the man whose name stands at the head of this article is proving himself precisely the right man for the times. In the absence of Gov. Fremont he has come to the front in a manner that shows him to be fully equal to the emergency which has thrust itself upon the executive department of the Territory (Apache problems). . . .

We are glad to be able to express what is not only our sentiment, but we believe also the sentiment of the people generally throughout the Territory, irrespective of party feeling, viz., that Mr. Gosper has acquitted himself in a manner highly creditable in this hour of our peril. The efficient service he has rendered will not be soon forgotten by the citizens of Arizona.

Los Angeles Times, May 15, 1913.

EX-GOVERNOR DIES; ALONE, PENNILESS. Unattended by relatives or friends and penniless, according to persons who knew him well, ex-Gov. J. J. Gosper of Arizona died yesterday afternoon at the County Hospital (Los Angeles). During the three days that former executive and once wealthy mining operator was at the institution he received no visitors.

Gosper had lived in Los Angeles almost a quarter of a century and had many friends and close acquaintances here. He was a prominent member of Bartlett-Logan Post, G.A.R. It appears that pride deterred him from communicating with his friends while he was at the County Hospital. Undoubtedly ample assistance would have been forthcoming from friends had his wants been known.

The fact that he went to the county institution instead of one of the private hospitals is taken by his acquaintances to indicate that he was without funds.

*   *   *

Wyatt spent almost fifty years in and around mining camps. Much of his time was in San Bernardino County, just west of the Colorado River. The following note, from the Prescott Courier, April 27, 1918, is but one indication of what he was doing.

Wyatt Earp, who is engaged in mining in the Whipple Mountains, was in Parker Monday. Mr. Earp has recently leased one of his mining properties, the Evening Star, to A. J. and Lester L. Munn. The lessees are working on quite an extensive scale and with very remunerative results.

*   *   *

The following is from the Quartz & Placer Claims, San Bernardino County, and is typical of Wyatt's many mining claim filings.

LOCATION NOTICE—QUARTZ CLAIM—NOTICE IS HEREBY GIVEN, That the undersigned citizen of the United States, over the age of twenty-one years, in compliance with the requirements of Chapter VI, Title 32 of the Revised Statutes of the United States, and the local customs, laws and regulations, has this day located and claim fifteen 1500 hundred lineal feet along the course of this land, lode or vein of mineral bearing quartz, and three hundred feet in width on each side of the middle of said lead, lode or vein

215

LOCATION NOTICE—Quartz Claim

Notice Is Hereby Given That the undersigned citizen____ of the United States, over the age of twenty-one years, in compliance with the requirements of Chapter VI, Title 32, of the Revised Statutes of the United States, and the local customs, laws and regulations, ha____ this day located and claimed ____ *Fifteen* ____ hundred linear feet along the course of this lead, lode or vein of mineral bearing quartz and ____ *Three* ____ hundred feet in width on each side of the middle of said lead, lode or vein, together with all mineral deposits contained therein, and all timber growing within the limits of said claim, and all water and water privileges thereon or appurtenant thereto, situate in the *Whipple* ____ Mining District,

County of San Bernardino, State of California, and more particularly described as follows, to-wit: *Commencing at this monument it being the initial monument Thence running three hundred feet Northeasterly Thence fifteen hundred feet Northwesterly Thence three hundred feet Southwesterly to North end center of Claims Thence three hundred feet Southwesterly Thence fifteen hundred feet Southeasterly Thence three hundred feet to Place of beginning. this mine is five miles north of Calzona del San Bernardino County California*

The date of discovery of this lead, lode or vein, is the *5* day of *March*, 192__ it is named and shall be known as the *Lancaster No 2.* Mine. Located *March 5* 192__.

Locator ____ *Wyatt Earp*

Witness: ____

No. *12*. "Endorsed": Recorded at request of *Locator Mar 13* 192_ at __ o. m. *9* a.m., in Book 143 of Mining Records, Page *372* ____ Records San Bernardino County.

FRANK W. SMITH, Junior P. O'Neill County Recorder,

by ____ *Fulton O'Neill* ____ Deputy Recorder, Fee $1.00.

A full, true and correct copy of the original.

FRANK W. SMITH County Recorder,

M. Eastman ____ Cora Beynis ____ Deputy Recorder

San Bernardino County Archives

together with all mineral deposits contained therein, and all timber growing within the limits of said claim, and all water and water privileges thereon or appurtenant thereto, situated in the Whipple Mining District, County of San Bernardino, State of California and more particularly described as follows, to-wit:

COMMENCING at this Monument it being the initial Monument thence three Hundred feet North Easterly thence fifteen Hundred feet North Westerly thence three Hundred feet South

216

Westerly to North westerly end of claim thence three Hundred feet Southwesterly thence fifteen Hundred feet South Easterly thence three Hundred feet North Easterly to place of beginning.

This claim is situated in the low foot hills of the Whipple Mountains and about one mile North of the six Mile post on the Needles road from the Colorado River and about five miles North from Calzona, San Bernardino County State of California.

The date of the discovery of this lead, lode or vein is the First day of July 1921; It is named and shall be known as the Frenchman mine. Located July the first, 1921.

Locator Wyatt Earp.

*   *   *

Wyatt's attempt to get his life story before the public, via film or books, was long and tortured. A few relevant excerpts from correspondence follow. This is from Wyatt to silent screen star William S. Hart, July 7, 1923; Earp Papers, Hart Collection, Natural History Museum, Los Angeles.

I was interested in what you told me of your plans for the next few years and the films that you are to make. I really had something of this in mind when Mrs. Earp and I called but you were busy and it is something for the moment that could wait.

During the past few years, many wrong impressions of the early days of Tombstone and myself have been created by writers who are not informed correctly, and this has caused me a concern which I feel deeply.

You know, I realize that I am not going to live to the age of Methuselah, and any wrong impression, I want made right before

I go away. The screen could do all this, I know, with yourself as the master mind. Not that I want to obligate you because of our friendship but I know that I can come to you with this and other things and not feel hurt at anything you may wish to say.

*   *   *

James Cooksey Earp, who had peddled drinks and run gambling tables in Arizona, Montana, Nevada, and California, spent his last years in Southern California. He died in Los Angeles on January 25, 1926. He had been in poor health, partly due to a severe arm-shoulder wound he had received in the Civil War. The following portion of a 1924 affidavit was provided by a neighbor, when James was trying to get additional pension aid; Civil War Pension File, National Archives.

Edward S. Johnson, being first duly sworn, deposes and says the he is of the age of 44 years, that his Post Office address is 340 Fourth St. in the City of San Bernardino, that the soldier, James C. Earp, resides on the premises occupied by affiant in a small building situated in the rear of affiant's residence, that said soldier has resided in said house and upon affiant's premises to affiant's knowledge since March 1922, that since the month of March, 1922, affiant has seen the soldier almost daily and has talked with him frequently and has observed his general physical and mental condition. . . .that said soldier suffered a stroke of paralysis on or about the first day of January 1923 which partially incapacitated him from administering to his own wants. He was unable to walk for six months during which time he was confined to his room and bed....at the present time said soldier is able to walk but is weak and in poor health and if not given attention would greatly neglect his care to such an extent that he would go without proper food and attention.

*   *   *

This letter, from Wyatt to Bill Hart on June 3, 1926, is another example of the Western lawman turning to Hollywood in order to create an ideal biography; Hart Papers, Natural History Museum, Los Angeles.

You can help me very much, I know; in the matter of publication particularly. There are the questions of the copyright and the royalty and the separation of the story rights from the picture, if you think it would be something worth while now, to have filmed.

You see, this experience is all new to me and I feel that I want to turn to you for advice.

*   *   *

Wyatt made a mistake, and put his publishing hopes in a friend and neighbor, John Flood, who as a writer matched Wyatt as a diplomat. Flood concocted Wyatt's "memoirs," in some of the West's worse prose. Hart tried to push Flood's concoction on all sorts of New York publishers, but every attempt led to rejection. Here are some words from Flood to Hart, February 19, 1926; Earp Papers, Hart Collection.

And I trust you will look kindly upon the first efforts of a novice, whose real purpose is to tell the story of Wyatt Earp, and who shall be pleased to be guided by anything you may have in mind to say.

*　*　*

The following excerpt, from the Thomas Y. Crowell Co. to William S. Hart, November 29, 1926, is typical of the reaction of the many publishers who staggered through the Flood manuscript; Earp Papers, Hart Collection.

To our mind, however, it contains more the source material for a story rather than the story itself. There is perhaps a trifle too much gun-play in it for the average reader who prefers his adventure diluted with other things. Frankly, also, we do not care particularly for the style in which the book is written. There is too much straining after effect. We are reluctantly declining the book and are returning it at Mr. Earp's request direct to you.

*　*　*

It is impossible to exaggerate the inferior quality of Flood's writing. Following are some passages of his account of the "Battle of Iron Springs," where Wyatt supposedly killed Curly Bill; from the Flood manuscript, Arizona Historical Society.

Crack! another hornet let loose, and Earp commenced to pull and tug.

Crack! Crack! "Don't let him get away fellows!" still the weapon was out of reach.

THOMAS Y. CROWELL COMPANY
PUBLISHERS
393 FOURTH AVENUE, NEW YORK

Nov. 29th, 1926

Mr. William S. Hart
6404 Sunset Boulevard
Hollywood, California

Dear Mr. Hart:

We have given very careful consideration to the life story of Mr. Wyatt Earp, and also have had in mind your cordial letter of commendation. We agree with you that the book is a fine pen picture of the west in the old frontier days.

To our mind, however, it contains more the source material for a story rather than the story itself. There is perhaps a trifle too much gun-play in it for the average reader who prefers his adventure diluted with other things. Frankly, also, we do not care particularly for the style in which the book is written. There is too much straining after effect.

We are reluctantly declining the book, and are returning it at Mr. Earp's request direct to you. Will you please communicate with him in our behalf and thank him for giving us this opportunity to consider it?

With regards, we remain

Very truly yours,

THOMAS Y. CROWELL COMPANY

JWM:OB

William S. Hart, cowboy star of the silent screen era, admired Wyatt, and they became fast friends. Hart tried for years to get Wyatt's biography in print. Natural History Museum, Los Angeles

Crack! Ah, he touched it with the tips of his fingers, closer, now he had it in his grasp. Crack! Crack! Crack! he started to return the fire.

Crack! Crack! Crack! they certainly were warming up.

Crack! Crack! Crack! he was giving them shot for shot, and scattering this way and that, they ran for the willows.

Once more his ammunition was gone and he reached for the horn of his saddle. Instantly, his horse was in the air; up and down, backwards and forwards he struggled, and then came the whine of the slugs.

Crack! Crack! Crack! ing! ing! ing! "Some one get him!" "Put him over the jumps!"

*   *   *

Hart took his friendship with Wyatt seriously and wrote to many publishers on his behalf. This is to Bobbs-Merrill Publishing Company, February 3, 1927; Hart Papers, Natural History Museum, Los Angeles.

I am sending today by prepaid express, a manuscript which I wish you would give the once over. There is no use in my telling you the value of such a work. Wyatt Earp is absolutely the very last of the great gun-men Peace Officers of the West. No true story of his life has even been written. Here is one.

If you find the book is not suitable for your handling, please return it to my, by express, charges collect.

*   *   *

Wyatt had reason to be suspicious of writers. Walter Noble Burns, author of Tombstone (1927) abused Wyatt's

223

confidence. Wyatt had given "his" story to John Flood, so he tried to steer Burns in other directions. Here is part of a letter from Wyatt to H. Maule, Doubleday, Page & Co., May 24, 1927; Burns Collection, University of Arizona.

I could see, of course, what a disappointment it must be to him, so, out of a friendly sympathy, I offered him the story of Bat Masterson. No, that was not just what he would fancy, but, after some deliberation, he expressed an inclination toward writing the story of Doc Holliday. Quite promptly, then, Mr. Burns left for Tombstone, Arizona. After that, over a period of six or eight months, I received several communications from him; upon each occasion with a request for information.

. . . .As I pondered over the matter, however, it appeared to me that the story of Doc Holliday had faded out and that the story was being built up more directly about myself. My surmises, therefore, were confirmed by your letter to me, under date of April 26th.

This I do not want. Anything to be published of such nature is sure to conflict with my own story, which is not ready yet for the press. . . .I am somewhat perplexed as to Mr. Burn's intentions. I would like to feel that there had been a mistake rather than that my wishes had been disregarded.

*　　*　　*

Flood's horrible prose meant the end of Wyatt's publishing plans via that route. Wyatt's biography would eventually be written by Stuart Lake. Here are portions of the first contact between them; Lake to Earp, December 25, 1927, and Earp to Lake, January 16, 1928, Lake Collection, Huntington Library.

224

John Flood, Wyatt's mining partner in the California desert and private secretary for twenty years. Good friend, awful writer. Truman Rex Fisher

225

What I'd like to do, what I have had in mind for a long time, is your biography, your memoirs if you prefer, working, of course, in collaboration with you and with material which you might furnish and shape—you to do the telling and I, the writing and whipping into shape. If you have not already come to an agreement with some one else in regard to such a book, I would appreciate very much a chance to discuss my idea with you.

Earp. Just what you say about your desire to write my biography is a question I cannot answer right at the present moment. I shall write you again about this but not sooner than six weeks or two months perhaps as I expect to leave within a few days for a trip out of the city. For several months, I have been confined to my bed with an attack of illness and I am just beginning to get on my feet again. Now I am planning a trip into the country (his mining claim, near Vidal) to build my health up, and after that I shall be able to interest myself in other things, I hope.

*   *   *

Among the many letters exchanged between Lake and Earp, several focused on Wyatt's gun play. Both of the following are excerpts from the Lake Collection, Huntington Library.

Lake to Earp, August 31, 1928.

In the first place, there have been printed about you the same sort of things that were printed about Bat—for example that Bat had killed thirty men when the truth is that he did in four. I want to be absolutely certain about your own career. As I have it now, there are the following:

Hoyt, in Dodge City
Two McLaurys and One Clanton in the street fight,
  some of these by Doc Holliday, one by Morg
The half-breed, Forentine at Pete Spence's Ranch
Frank Stilwell, at Tucson
Curly Bill at Iron Springs
Were there any others? Either before Tombstone or later, in
the San Francisco, Alaska, Nevada or Colorado days?

Earp to Lake, September 13, 1928.

I do not remember the name of the milliner who witnessed the
street fight in Tombstone. In that affair, Billy Clanton and Frank
McLowry had four or five bullet holes in their bodies, and of
course it would be impossible to declare who was responsible for
the shots. I was responsible for none of the others only those
names which I already have given you.

*   *   *

**One of the most controversial aspects of Wyatt's career
was his showdown with Ben Thompson in Ellsworth,
Kansas, in 1873. Not a shred of evidence exists to show
Wyatt anywhere near the scene; in fact, the case, of
disarming Ben Thompson, is very well documented, and
Wyatt had no role in it. As an elderly man, though, he
claimed otherwise. Here is a portion of his letter to Lake of
November 30, 1928, in which he discusses several early
incidents; Lake Collection, Huntington Library.**

Charles Hatton is quite correct concerning the several incidents about which you wrote me. In the one affair, the fellow King

227

(a sergeant in the United States Army) had gotten a furlow, or a leave of absence, had bought a week's supply of food and a new suite of clothes, and had come to Wichita, and, of course, he was very friendly with the cowboy element. When I appear on the scene, he was surrounded by a large crowd. He was flourishing a gun and boating in loud tones what he would do to Wyatt Earp. He was only about fifty feet from me when I turned the corner of the street. Without hesitation, I stepped up to him, for I discerned immediately that he was a big bluffer, and I disarmed him while he still was flourishing the gun; much to the surprise of the crowd (of about 150 persons) which expected to see me shot dead. This King is the man whom Bat Masterson Killed about a year of so later at Sweetwater.

In the other affair, the man's name was George Peshaw (pronounced "Pa-shaw" -I am not sure the spelling is correct). He was a Texas gambler, and also friendly with the cowboy element. I had some little trouble with him in Elsworth, at the time that I arrested Ben Thompson; about which latter affair, he twitted me considerably.

*　　*　　*

Wyatt's sense of irony comes through in this portion of his letter to Lake of November 30, 1928, regarding the Tombstone shootout; Lake Collection.

Recently, a friend of Mr. Flood purchased a copy of Mr. Breakenridge's story "Helldorado." It is poorly written, he said, and in the story of the street fight, Mr. Breakenridge tells that the Clantons and the McLowerys were unarmed and that they threw up their hands. All of which is very interesting, and probably explains how Virgil Earp, Morgan Earp and Doc Holliday were wounded during the fight.

*　　*　　*

Wyatt fumed about Breakenridge's treachery in Helldorado. In the 1920s, Breakenridge was an investigator into the Lotta Crabtree case, and had cultivated Wyatt, in order to get Wyatt to testify about the Tombstone boom days. This portion of a letter from Wyatt to Lake of November 6, 1928, leaves no question as to Wyatt's opinion of Breakenridge; Lake Papers.

B did not mention in his book I don't suppose, that his good friend Johnny Behan was arrested while holding the Sheriffs office for malfeasance in office and just got away with it by the skin of his teeth—The records will show for itself. I never wore a steel vest, and never had such a thing in my possession. Another one of his *dam lies*. I can't just understand him. As he has always of late years seemed friendly towards me. I have some of his letters where he claims that he will not roast me in his book. As I have written and told him that he must be very careful what he puts in print about me—He is a sly fox of the worst kind, and naturally feels sure because I told Behan and his so called brave men which were his deputies and Breakenridge being one of them. And when they came to arrest me I just laughed at them and told them to just run away—And he holds that up against me. If there was ever a mean contemptible persons he certainly is the one—Just imagine a man to come to you for favors? which he has done, and then to be so treacherous.

229

*　　*　　*

Newton J. Earp died near Sacramento on December 18, 1928. The following extract, from a lengthy article in the Sacramento Union of January 25, 1976, suggests that Newton's descendants were irritated and resentful of all the publicity garnered by "Uncle Wyatt."

While all this was going on, Newton helped to found the Methodist Church of Garden City, Kansas. He was also elected the first city marshal there.

Following many years of farming, the Newton Earp family moved to a ranch at Paradise Valley, Nevada. In 1898, Nancy Jane died. . . . For a time, Newton lived at the Veteran's Home in Napa County, but again moved to Sacramento, living in the Fruitridge area. . . .Newton, who had served on numerous "peace committees" to keep law and order in pioneering Kansas communities, remained active in church work, his good deeds never making the newspapers.

Newton has several children living in Sacramento. Mrs. Alice Wells, W. Clyde and V. Edwin Earp. The last to survive was Virgil Edwin, who died in 1959 in Vallejo. The youngest child, he achieved some fame in the 1950s when he won $32,000 in a nationally televised quiz show.

While Newton remained content to live out his life in peace and quiet in Sacramento, Wyatt sought writers to tell them a version of his "famous life." Of the original 10 children, finally only Wyatt and Newton remained.

In 1928, Wyatt finally found an author for his tales of the West. Perhaps he knew the fictionalized book by biographer Lake would make him a hero.

Who was there left to contradict him? Brother Newton had recently died at 91 plus.

*   *   *

Shortly before Wyatt's death, his friend Tex Rickard died. Wyatt and Tex operated adjacent saloons in Nome in 1900-1901, and met again later when Tex became a leading saloon owner and fight promoter in Goldfield, Nevada. When Tex went on to national fame as a fight promoter, he and Wyatt kept in touch; from a letter to Wm. S. Hart, January 7, 1929, Earp Papers, Hart Collection.

This morning's newspapers announce the passing of Tex Rickard. Poor Tex - it seems sad that he should be cut down, or his years cut short, just at the time when life was at its full tide; such is the fate that happens to many men when they are going strong. He surely made a success as a fight promoter; one of the best in history. Jack Dempsey has lost his best friend; no one will take the interest in him that Rickard did. . . .Only to move back ten years! that would be worth a world fortune. But it can't be done now; I will have to be satisfied for the ten years that are ahead -and that's a mighty lot. And I can't plan anymore to climb the hills and hit the drill.

*   *   *

Wyatt Earp died at his home in Los Angeles on January 13, 1929. His obituary appeared throughout most of the nation's newspapers. Following is a portion of the Los Angeles Times of January 17, 1929, which featured the funeral ceremonies.

231

Wyatt Earp's funeral was conducted down at Pierce Brothers' chapel yesterday and it was like a reunion of the sturdy men and women who knew Wyatt as a wiry, six-foot two-gun officer of the law in mining town, cow camp and almost anywhere along the frontier where trouble was apt to pop loose.

George M. Easton came in from Colton, recalling that it was the Earp boys were called into Colton to help clean up that town at a time when outlawry was so rampant that desperadoes used to ride into town at night and knock out the lamps in houses with their guns.

Bill Hart, no novice in the ways of the West himself, came in from his place and was one of the pallbearers. Bill, as a little boy, knew Wyatt in Dodge City when that town was going good on the frontier. Tom Mix was there and as a friend of the deceased was a pall-bearer. . . .

Maj. John P. Clum, one of the well-known figures of the West of earlier days, was one of the pall-bearers. Maj. Clum is a long-time friend of the Earps. Why, he was the first Mayor of Tombstone and Wyatt Earp was his Chief of Police. . . .

Wilson Mizner, another pallbearer, and J. P. Browner, knew Earp up in the Klondike country, also. They met Maj. Clum again, for the first time since then, at the funeral yesterday. Other pallbearers included George W. Parsons, formerly of Tombstone, Charles Welch, Fred Dornberger and Jim Mitchell.

Out from the colorful past of the old West stepped these friends of Wyatt Earp, their numbers increased by others until extra chairs had to be brought into the chapel to seat them all. There they sat, this colorful company of actors from the melo-drama of the older days, bronzed of face, and those who were not white haired were bald headed. Many of them carried canes and they were not for mere ornament, either. Some wore business suits and some wore heavy jackets of wool or leather; some with large

Pallbearers at Wyatt Earp's funeral included such notables as George Parsons and John Clum, holding hats, standing next to Bill Hart; actor Tom Mix is far right. Natural History Museum, Los Angeles

long overcoats made to "turn the wind" that has a habit of driving the chill into the bones when one is getting old. There was a sprinkling of younger folks there, too.

Sitting there in the chapel before Wyatt's bier banked high with flowers, while from somewhere came the music of a harp, these men and women no doubt let their thoughts drift back to the happy, though turbulent days when the man in the casket there before them was among them helping to lay the foundations for the West of today.

When Dr. Harper of the Wilshire Boulevard Congregational Church began to speak, these veterans snapped out of their reverie and leaned forward. Some of them rested their elbows on their canes, as they cupped their hands over their ears.

*   *   *

Stuart Lake put in correspondence what he could not put in Wyatt Earp: Frontier Marshal. In this letter of February 13, 1930, to Ira Rich Kent, of Houghton, Mifflin Co., Lake tells what he knows of Wyatt's wife, Josephine "Sadie" Marcus Earp; from the Houghton Collection, Harvard University Archives.

Mrs. Earp, as that lady now is known and has been for forty-nine years, went to Tombstone from San Francisco with the first rush, to work the dancehalls of that camp. Bat Masterson, and a score of oldtimers, have told me that she was the belle of the honkytonks, the prettiest dame in three hundred or so of her kind. Johnny Behan was a notorious "chaser" and a free spender making lots of money. He persuaded the beautiful Sadie to leave the honkytonk and set her up as his "girl," after which she was known in Tombstone as Sadie Behan. Wyatt Earp was in Tombstone, but

234

Wyatt's record, in Dodge, for example, was that he steered pretty clear of entangling alliances. However, in Tombstone Wyatt fell for Sadie and Sadie for him. There apparently is some doubt with those who were their intimates as to which did the "propositioning" but the first thing Johnny Behan knew, Wyatt had his girl who thenceforth was known to Tombstone as Sadie Earp. (Now, none of this is hearsay; every word is authenticated history, much of record.) In other matters of purely personal nature, Wyatt bested Johnny Behan at every turn but one, a turn to which Behan later admitted under oath and in which he double-crossed Wyatt. Even this turned out to Wyatt's advantage tremendously in the long run. Behan, to cite another instance, opened a farobank and on the first night it essayed business Wyatt went against it and broke the bank—Johnny as well. But, that did not rankle one-tenth as much as Behan's resentment over the loss of his girl. . . .It has occured to me that I might tell of the girl affair without mentioning any names. Am I to do that or very carefully avoid it? In a way it is absolutely essential to the status of my work with those who know. I will admit that I might leave it out entirely, and lose caste with only those whose regard I value most, as far as this job is concerned. Which is why I'd like to have your opinion.

* * *

Earp, Hart, and Lake left voluminous correspondence relating to the efforts to get Earp's biography published. The book did appear, two years after Wyatt's death, so there is no telling what his reaction to it would have been. However, Ira Rich Kent, from Houghton, Mifflin, had grave reservations about Lake's prose, as comes through in his letter to Lake of August 30, 1929; Lake Papers, Huntington Library.

Josephine, Mrs. Wyatt Earp, in 1931, when Stuart Lake's biography of Wyatt appeared. Truman Rex Fisher

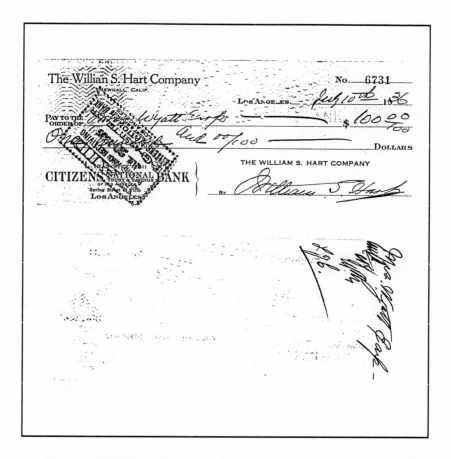

The check reads:

The William S. Hart Company
NEWHALL, CALIF.
No. 6731
LOS ANGELES July 10th 1936
PAY TO THE ORDER OF Wyatt Earp
One Hundred 00/100 $ 100 00/100
DOLLARS

CITIZENS NATIONAL BANK
HEAD OFFICE 7811
TRUST & SAVINGS
OF LOS ANGELES
Spring Street at Fifth
LOS ANGELES

THE WILLIAM S. HART COMPANY
By William S. Hart

Years after Wyatt's death, Bill Hart retained a relationship with Mrs. Earp. Hart Collection, Natural History Museum, Los Angeles

We think the story of Wyatt Earp is one of unquestioned interest and we see no reason why you should not be entirely competent to tell it, equipped as you are with writing ability, with an enthusiasm for accuracy and with the cooperation of Mrs. Earp as well as that of Earp himself. . . .In the long quotations from Earp himself we have found a little lack of Western flavor and freedom.

237

Did he really talk in this rather literary and polysyllabic style, or have you, perhaps unconsciously, smoothed out his speech to an undue degree?

*   *   *

Lake's methods are explained in a letter to Burton Rascoe, January 9, 1941; Lake Papers, Huntington Library.

As a matter of cold fact, Wyatt never dictated a word to me. I spent hours and days and weeks with him—and I wish you could see my notes! I had to pump him for all the details. He knew information, but none of which he handed out in any sort of narrative form. . . .There had been such an erroneous matter printed about the Earp exploits, none ever put down in the order of cause and effect, that I was hunting for a method which would stamp mine as authentic. Possibly it was a form of "cheating." But, when I came to the task, I decided to employ the direct quotation form sufficiently often to achieve my purpose. I've often wondered if I did not overdo in this respect.

*   *   *

In light of the above—"Wyatt never dictated a word to me"—consider the following prose which Lake hath wrought. This is from a Saturday Evening Post article of November 1, 1930, on gunfighters. The narrator is Wyatt Earp.

I considered myself a fair hand with pistol, rifle or shotgun, and I could make a creditable showing in target matches, but I learned more about gun fighting from Tom Speers' cronies during the summer of '71 that I had ever dreamed was in the book. Those fellows took their gun play seriously; which was only to be expected, in view of the conditions under which they lived. Shooting, to them, was considerably more than aiming at a mark and pulling a trigger. Models of weapons, methods of wearing them, means of getting them into action and of operating them, all to the one end of combining high speed with absolute accuracy, contributed to the frontiersman's shooting skill. The sought-after degree of proficiency was that which could turn to most effective account the split second between life and death. Hours upon hours of practice and wide experience in the actualities of the art supported the arguments over style.

*　　*　　*

In 1931 the New York Times published an article debunking Bill Tilghman, and other Western heroes. Wyatt's widow, Josephine, asked John Flood to clarify matters, which he did in a letter to the New York Times of June 21, 1931. In the excerpts which follow, it becomes evident how closely Flood worked with both Wyatt and Josephine.

Mrs. Wyatt Earp has just handed me a clipping from the NEW YORK TIMES, the caption of which is "Woman of Old West 'Debunks' Its Legends."

It seems, according to the article before me, that a Mrs. Anna Anderson, now dead, was responsible for the tale that the "famous Bill Tilghman fled in one of her dresses after hiding under her feather bed, because he feared Wyatt Earp would kill him."

I had not heard that one before; it was all new to me, and very interesting. You know, for the past twenty-five years I have functioned as Wyatt Earp's secretary, and since his death on Jan. 13, 1929, I have served his widow, Mrs. Josephine S. Earp, in a

239

similar capacity.

As I recollect, some ten years ago, Mr. Tilghman visited Los Angeles. He was showing a film at that time, the story of his career. There was no hesitation whatever on the part of Wyatt Earp in extending a cordial greeting. During Mr. Tilghman's stay the two men were constantly in each other's company and every evidence of an old friendship was manifest. Mrs. Earp was introduced to Mr. Tilghman and Mr. Tilghman invited us all to dinner.

I have the stenographic notes of the story of Wyatt Earp, just as Mr. Earp dictated them to me a few years ago. I fail to find any mention of a Mrs. Anderson. On the other hand, Mr. Earp had spoken to me of Mr. Tilghman on many occasions, and always in words of friendship and praise. Had there ever been any enmity between the two men I am sure the fact would have been made known to me over this long period of years, as Mr. Earp repeated to me many incidents of a confidential nature which never shall appear for publication.

*   *   *

Nothing in print about Wyatt pleased his wife Josephine, and this did not change after Wyatt's death. Short stories, novels, even Lake's biography infuriated her, even though she had participated in the research to some degree. She went to Wm. Hunsaker, former Tombstone attorney who was practicing in Los Angeles and occasionally did some legal work for the Earps. This is from Hunsaker to Mrs. Wyatt S. Earp, January 15, 1931; Ellsworth Collection, Arizona Historical Society.

Your loyalty to Wyatt and your efforts to protect his memory have been gratifying to me and you have my sincere sympathy.

Explorer Lincoln Ellsworth was a boyhood fan of Wyatt Earp, and named his vessel in his honor. The "Wyatt Earp" in the 1930s took expeditions to the Arctic Ocean and to Antarctica. Natural History, July-August, 1934

However, there is no way in which you, *as his widow and heir*, can obtain any redress, either by way of injunction or damages.

After you left the office yesterday I spent considerable time in looking up the authorities, thinking possibly Mr. Wright and I had been wrong in concluding you could do nothing, but, unfortunately, the authorities confirm the opinions Mr. Wright and I had expressed to you. It is universally held by the courts that the relatives and heirs of a dead person are not entitled to sue, either for damages or injunctive relief, for defamation of the memory of a deceased relative.

*   *   *

More than the printed word bothered Wyatt's widow. The following to Mrs. Earp is from A. H . Gardner, Chamber of Commerce, Tombstone, July 17, 1931, and needs no comment; Hart Papers, Natural History Museum, Los Angeles.

In reply to your letter of june 9th, I do not think that you have any grounds for objecting to the Earp Clanton battle as given yearly at the Helldorado for the reason that it is history and reenacted just as it happened and I want to further say that nothing in it reflects on your late husband, and I also want to say that personally I am of the opinion that your husband was a clean, courageous man. . . .he has many friends here and I have yet to find with one exception any one who did not accord him as a brave man.

*   *   *

Los Angeles Times, December 21, 1944.

EARP WIDOW'S RITES PLANNED

Funeral arrangements for Mrs. Josephine Marcus Earp, 75, widow of the picturesque western gun-fighter, U. S. Marshall Wyatt Earp, were being completed yesterday by relatives. Mrs. Earp died Tuesday (December 19) of a heart attack at her home at 1812 W. 48th St.

Mrs. Earp was at her husband's side in the days when the famous peace officer was restoring law and order from Dodge City to Tombstone. The couple came to Los Angeles shortly after the turn of the century to make their home. Earp died here January 13, 1929.

Among Mrs. Earp's survivors is a sister-in-law, Mrs. Virgil Earp of San Bernardino.

* * *

Mrs. Virgil Earp—Allie to her friends—outlived her husband by more than forty years. She died in Los Angeles on November 14, 1947. This obituary is from the Phoenix Gazette of November 15.

Funeral services will be conducted Monday for Mrs. Virgil Earp, 98, last member of the famed law enforcement family of western frontier days, who died at her home yesterday.

A native of Council Bluffs, Ia., she was married 61 years ago in Omaha, Neb., to Virgil Earp of Tombstone fame. He was a member of the family that included U. S. Marshal Wyatt Earp and his deputies and brothers, Morgan and Virgil, who cleaned out the Clanton gang.

Since the death of her husband 40 years ago, Mrs. Earp had lived here with her grandniece, Mrs. C. E. Halliwell.

243

*   *   *

Newton Earp, oldest of the Earp boys, had a son named Virgil, who was born in 1880. Virgil became famous as a television game-show whiz. He died on November 20, 1959; the following obituary, dated November 21, is in the Earp Collection, Colton Public Library.

Old age brought down yesterday the last of the fighting Earps.

Virgil Earp, only living child of the six Earp boys, most famous of who was Marshal Wyatt Earp, died peacefully at the age of 80. His father was Wyatt's brother Newton.

Virgil got nationwide attention in 1958 when he appeared on the television quiz show, "The $64,000 question," and won $32,000 in the Wild West category.

It was a category he had lived out—birth in a wagon train's camp ground at Tombstone, Ariz.; a toter of a six-shooter when he was 16; sheriff of Paradise Valley, Nev., when he was 18, and claimant of three notches in his gun by the time he was 21, and eventually a gambling hall operator known among gamblers as a man of his word.

Recently he showed a newsman his .38 Colt he inherited from an uncle.

"We Earps never know when someone out of the past will come looking for us," he said.

"We had to kill a lot of men as lawmen and memories are long in the West."

The first man Virgil killed, he once said, had molested his sister.

In 1893, some men gunned down Wyatt's brother, Morgan, at Tombstone. Wyatt went on a vengeance spree, getting five men. Virgil said he and his uncle Wyatt went into Mexico, across the

244

border from Nogales, Ariz., in 1903 and got his last two. Wyatt shot down Pete Spence. Virgil, then 24, killed Indian Charlie.

Just before he went on the television quiz show, Virgil told an interviewer:

"A woman was safer in the Wild West than she would be today in midtown Manhattan. In the old days there was no such thing as juvenile delinquency, no house robberies and no organized government. There was just good men and bad men—and one policy, "a life for a life."

Virgil died at the home of his niece, Mrs. Frank McKenzie, of Vallejo. Surviving is his daughter, Mrs. Alice Wright of Kelseyville, Lake County, Calif.

Recently during the furor over rigged television quizzes, someone asked Earp if by any chance he had been coached in his TV appearances.

He snorted an indignant "No."

"Who," he asked, "could tell me anything about the West?"

*   *   *

Hildreth (Mrs. Charles) Halliwell, Allie Earp's grand-niece, spent more than thirty years in the midst of the Earp clan. She was raised with the Virgil Earp family in Prescott, and while living in Los Angeles from 1910 through the 1940s, she took care of James, who died in 1926, and Allie, who died in 1947. Following are some abstracts and excerpts of her knowledge and impressions of various Earps; from H. Halliwell Interviews, University of Arizona.

(Describe Virgil) I last saw him when I was six. He was large, jolly, I adored him. Easy to know and like. I never saw him mad or angry.

245

(Describe Wyatt) I knew him for years, but mostly when he was an elderly man. He was tall, quiet, more slender than Virg, straight carriage. Never talked much, never talked about the past. Used to talk to Allie when he would come to our house for supper. They got along well enough, but there was some reserve between them.

(Describe James) I only knew him when he was an old man. He talked alot, but I don't remember details of his western yarns. Lived a year with me, died in my house. His wife—he referred to her as Bessie. Had two children, but I never saw or knew them.

(Describe the dealings with author Frank Waters) He interviewed Allie many times, for many hours, in my home. I cannot explain the anti-Earp material in his books. "He wrote lies." Allie was shown a draft of some of Waters writings. She threatened to sue him if he published that "bunch of lies." She told this to me many times.

(Allie and Virgil) They were devoted to each other. Up and down economically, but nothing mattered to them as long as they were together. He was a marshal, gambler, had a little ranch in Kirkland Valley, did some prospecting, was a stage rider. My mother met my father in Vanderbilt, where Uncle Virg operated Earp's Hall. My mom talked a lot about Vanderbilt. My mother had come from Kansas to live with Virg and Aunt Allie, met my father there (Vanderbilt), and they got married in Los Angeles.

(What about Mattie, Wyatt's wife?) She was loved by Allie. She was a suicide because of Wyatt taking up with Sadie.

(Drinking, gambling) Were Wyatt and Virg heavy drinkers? Not that I knew about, but maybe in their younger years they were. Were they honest gamblers? I suppose, "especially Uncle Virg."

*   *   *

246

Fame, time, and the help of Wyatt Earp combined to obscure his background. The following is the entry in Who Was Who In America, Vol. IV, 1961-68.

EARP, WYATT BERRY STAPP, marshall; b. Monmouth, Ill., Mar. 19, 1848; s. Nicholas and Virginia (Cooksey) E.; married, 1868; m. 2d, Josephine Sarah Marcus, circa 1897; no children. Moved with family to Cal., 1864; drove stagecoach between San Bernardino and Los Angeles, 1865; drove coaches to Ariz. and Utah, 1865-67, later worked as buffalo hunter, horse handler for railroads; hunter for U. S. Govt. surveyors in Kan., Okla., Tex., 1870-71; independent buffalo hunter, 1871-73; earned reputation for bravery and skill with firearms; marshall of Ellsworth, Kan., 1873; dep. marshall Wichita, Kan., 1874-76, Dodge City, Kan., 1876, 77-79; dep. sheriff Cochise County (Ariz.) at Tombstone, 1879-82, marshall, 1882; led brothers Virgil and Morgan and Doc Holliday against Ike Clanton's band in battle of O. K. Corral, Tombstone, 1881; after retirement from law enforcement, lived off real estate, oil, mining investment and gambling. Died Los Angeles, Jan. 13, 1929.

In this one paragraph, therefore, appear more than a dozen inaccuracies or exaggerations. The most obvious ones are the confusions over marriages, crediting Wyatt with any role at Ellsworth, confusing Cochise with Pima County, branding Ike as leader of a "band," and giving Wyatt, rather than Virgil, the credit for being in charge in Tombstone. His "real estate, oil, mining" income was less than meager, as for the last ten years of his life he and Josephine were almost in a hand-to-mouth mode.

However, as confusing and erroneous as is the above

247

Wyatt presented this photograph to movie actor William S. Hart in 1923, at the beginning of their close friendship. Natural History Museum, Los Angeles

A view of Wyatt's oil property in Kern County, California, as developed by Getty Oil Company in the 1980s. Truman Rex Fisher

entry in **Who Was Who In America**, Wyatt was not the sole culprit. In the years since the Tombstone shootout, truth had blended with mystery, exaggeration, wish-fulfillment, and a fascination with the West. Two years after Wyatt's death, Stuart Lake's biography would give Wyatt a strong push towards the halls of legend. As the century wore on, books, magazines, movies, and television portrayals would present to the world an Earp family which bore little resemblance to the Earps who, while often wearing badges, toiled, drank, gambled, mined, and wandered the West in the last part of the nineteenth century.

SOURCES

A detailed "Earpiana" bibliography would take a small pamphlet. Listed below are only those manuscripts, documents, collections, and publications that have been used in this book.

MANUSCRIPTS

Berkeley, Bancroft Library: Bancroft biog. files of Virgil & Wyatt Earp.

Butte, Montana, Butte-Silver Bow Archives: City Police Files.

Cambridge, Mass., Harvard Law School Library: Crabtree Case File.

Cambridge, Mass., Harvard University Archives: Houghton Collection.

Carson City, Nevada Historical Society: misc. Earp documents.

Colton, California, Public Library: Earp Research Collection.

Columbia, Missouri, State Historical Society: Barton County Records.

Juneau, Alaska State Museum: Earp Clippings.

Los Angeles, Natural History Museum, Seaver Center: William S. Hart Papers.

McLean, Virginia, U. S. Marshals Collection: Dake-Earp Files.

Monmouth, Illinois, Earp Birthplace Museum: Earp Family Papers.

Monmouth, Illinois, Warren County Library: Earp Research Papers.

New York, New-York Historical Society Archives: W. McLaury Letters.

Pella, Iowa, Central College, Archives: Earp Collection.

Phoenix, State Archives: Yavapai County Court Records.

Prescott, Sharlot Hall Museum: biographical and miscellaneous files.

San Bernardino County, California: Mining Claims.

San Francisco, Wells, Fargo History Room: Wells, Fargo Collection.

San Marino, Huntington Library: Stuart Lake Collection; Fred Dodge Collection.

Springfield, Illinois, Illinois State Archives: Civil War Records.

Tombstone, Cochise County: Court Records.

Tucson, Arizona Historical Society: Lincoln Ellsworth Collection; John Flood Manuscript; Medigovitch Collection; Tombstone Common Council Minutes.

Tucson, University of Arizona: Walter Noble Burns Papers; John Clum Papers; Hildreth Halliwell Interviews.

Washington, D. C., National Archives: Earp Military Records, Mexican War, Civil War.

BOOKS

Bartholomew, Ed. *Wyatt Earp: The Untold Story*.Toyahvale, Texas, 1963.

Boyer, Glenn. *The Suppressed murder of Wyatt Earp*. San Antonio, 1976.

252

Colusa County, California. San Francisco, 1880.

Dodge, Fred. *Under Cover for Wells Fargo*. Boston, 1969.

Martin, Douglas. *Tombstone's Epitaph*.Albuquerque, 1951.

Masterson, W. A. (Bat). *Famous Gunfighters of the Western Frontier*. Ruidoso, New Mexico,1959; orig. pub. New York, 1907.

Parsons, George. *The Private Journal of George W. Parsons*. Phoenix, 1939.

Turner, Alford. *The Earps Talk*.College Station, Texas, 1980.

Turner, Alford. *The O. K. Corral Inquest*.College Station, Texas, 1981.

Waters, Frank. *The Earp Brothers of Tombstone*. New York, 1960.

Who Was Who in America, IV, 1961-68. Chicago, 1968.

Winters, Wayne. *Forgotten Mines and Treasures of the Great Southwest*. Tombstone, 1972.

ARTICLES

Bishop, Wm. Henry. "Across Arizona."
Harper's Monthly, LXVI (March, 1883), 493-502.

Clum, John. "It All Happened in Tombstone."
Arizona Historical Review, II (October, 1929), 46-72.

McClenahan, Judith. "Call and See the Elephant."
Idaho Yesterdays, XI (Fall, 1967), 11-13.

Roberts, Gary (ed.). "Gunfight at O.K. Corral: The Wells Spicer Decision." *Montana Magazine of History*, XX (January, 1970, 62-74.

"Rousseau Diary: Across the Desert to California, from Salt Lake to San Bernardino in 1864." *Quarterly, San Bernardino County Museum Association*, VI (Winter, 1958), 1-17.

NEWSPAPERS

Colton Chronicle
Colton *Semi-Tropic*
Dodge City *Times*
Florence *Arizona Enterprise*
Ford County Globe
Kansas City *Journal*
Los Angeles Herald
Los Angeles Times
Monmouth, Ill. *Daily Review Atlas*
Nome Daily News
Needle's Eye
New York Times
Nome Gold Digger
Phoenix *Arizona Gazette*
Phoenix *Arizona Republican*
Phoenix Gazette
Phoenix *Herald*
Portland Oregonian
Prescott *Arizona Journal-Miner*
Prescott *Arizona Miner*
Prescott *Enterprise*
Riverside *Morning Enterprise*
San Bernardino *Daily Courier*
San Bernardino *Daily Times*
San Bernardino *Kaleidoscope*
San Bernardino *Sun*
San Bernardino *Sun-Telegram*
San Bernardino *Weekly Chronicle*
San Diego *Daily Sun*
San Diego *Union*
San Francisco *Daily Examiner*

San Luis Obispo *Tribune*
Tombstone *Epitaph*
Tombstone *Nugget*
Tombstone *Prospector*
Tonopah Bonanza
Tonopah Miner
Tonopah *Sun*
Tucson *Arizona Weekly Citizen*
Tucson *Star*
Wichita City Eagle
Wichita Weekly Beacon

OTHER

Chafin, Carl (ed.). "The West of George Whitwell Parsons," typescripts of several of the annual diaries of Parsons; I have used those of 1881-1883. Copies of these typescripts have been bound and are with the original diaries in the Library, Arizona Historical Society, Tucson.

Jones, Clark Harding. "A History of the Development and Progress of Colton, California." M. A. Thesis, Claremont Graduate School, 1951, copy in Colton Public Library.

United States Census, 1880, Tombstone, Pima County, Arizona.

INDEX

257